The
Parables of Conflict
in Luke

BOOKS BY J. STANLEY GLEN
Published by The Westminster Press

The Parables of Conflict in Luke
The Recovery of the Teaching Ministry

The
Parables of Conflict
in Luke

by

J. STANLEY GLEN

Philadelphia
THE WESTMINSTER PRESS

LIBRARY OF CONGRESS CATALOG CARD No. 62–9811

PRINTED IN THE UNITED STATES OF AMERICA

Contents

Foreword

These expositions originated out of an appreciation of the evangelical potentialities of the parables peculiar to Luke. Several arose from sermons revised repeatedly because the respective parables seemed to possess unusual relevance. But most arose out of an awareness that here was Biblical material which to a surprising extent already fulfilled the objectives set forth in Bultmann's well-known proposal. Its freedom from apocalyptic forms and its emphasis on the use of critical human situations for purposes of communication were the features that contributed to this awareness. In this respect, the material exemplifies Jesus' adaptation of the best-known language of all— scenes from everyday life involving basic problems of human existence—for the interpretation of his mission and message. This he accomplishes with a minimum of formal, kerygmatic terminology. Such a procedure is not without significance for the theology and practice of evangelism in the present day.

The introduction suggests the approach adopted in the expositions that follow. The expositions are arranged according to a theological pattern. The first two are concerned with the divine initiative, the next four with various forms of spiritual need, and the last four with the meaning of faith and of discipleship. The synopsis deals

7

with the principal issues and serves to tie the expositions together. At every stage there has been an effort to relate these issues to the ideological perspectives of modern life.

Among the various commentaries and studies of the parables to which the writer is indebted, mention should be made of *The Parables of Jesus*, by Joachim Jeremias. Gratitude should also be expressed for the courtesies extended by The Westminster Press and particularly by Dr. Paul L. Meacham, Religious Book Editor. Finally, a word of gratitude is appropriate for my wife, Winifred, whose faith and interest in Biblical theology have always been such an inspiration to me.

J. S. G.

I

Introduction

An impression prevails that the parables of Jesus are, on the whole, simple stories with rather obvious meanings. Each parable is presumed to contain a familiar moral, consistent with common sense and respectability, and accessible to anyone possessed of both. It is especially so with the popular impression of the parables peculiar to Luke, since they more than others have the appearance of illustrations of goodness rather than of difficult stories requiring explanation.[1] The parable of the good Samaritan, for instance, is presumed to emphasize a form of charity, and the parable of the prodigal son a form of self-improvement suggestive of a prosaic moralism that almost anyone could comprehend without Christ and even without faith in God. It is apparently that simple. But it is at this point that doubts begin to arise about the adequacy of such an interpretation. The interpretation is too flat and lifeless to be convincing. A feeling emerges that Christ would never have been crucified for such facile teaching. Had he been only a purveyor of pious maxims, there never would have been any cross.

A different impression may be obtained, however, with the parables laid side by side, for the sake of seeing them as a whole and detecting their common features. For it will be recognized that they are all stories of critical hu-

9

man situations. They portray scenes from everyday life in first-century Palestine so varied and representative in character that they amount to a panorama of the common problems of the people. From this perspective they are not flat and lifeless. They are serious. They possess a life-and-death (existential) quality that immediately captures our interest. There is a beaten, half-dead man by the side of the road; a reckless, wayward son returning home; a despairing tax collector at prayer; a diseased beggar at the entrance of a wealthy home; a rich farmer suddenly dying; an unscrupulous manager exposed; a widow pleading with a dishonest judge; a ruler planning to attack his neighbor. Sounding suspiciously similar to a review of current events, this list could be duplicated in modern life and regarded as a description of the human predicament.

Nevertheless, the parables of Luke present more than a panorama of the everyday problems of first-century Palestine. Their dramatic realism, though fascinating, was not intended as a social analysis that would leave us more problems than answers. For it is possible to magnify the human predicament out of all proportion, so that it obscures the ultimate purpose of the parables. Moreover, even a meager understanding of the mission of Jesus will be enough to indicate that he came with answers rather than problems, and was indeed, himself, the answer to the human predicament.

A closer scrutiny will therefore reveal that the parables really portray less of the human than of the divine. The critically human problem will recede before the eminence of the divine answer. Instead of a life lived in the shadow of a question mark, it will be a life lived in the image of God. For the parables' primary concern is with him, whose existence defines the real center of religion and of human life, and is of such importance in the great war of ideas and loyalties that pervades the whole of the modern world. In one way or another they all bear upon this one, fundamental theme, so that each parable is only a different variation upon the theme. In other words, their orientation is theocentric.

This is most clearly illustrated in the theme of the divine initiative commonly recognized in the parables of the lost sheep, the lost coin, and the prodigal son. It is implied in the theme "humble-exalted," which so aptly represents the dimension within which most of the parables are designed. For how can these two qualities be adequately defined, except in relation to God as the normative reference point? The same orientation is evident in the parable of the rich farmer whose plans for a pleasurable retirement were suddenly interrupted by death. The problem central to his life was his indifference to God, which would be better known today as "practical atheism." With the Pharisee in the Temple, the problem was not so different from that of the rich farmer. His egotistic prayer, revealing a life that revolved around itself, also revealed that his problem was at the center. For with all his religion, he did not really know what it meant to believe in God. Even in the case of the good Samaritan, the radical love exemplified cannot be understood apart from that love toward God which is offered with the whole heart, soul, strength, and mind. The one love is integral to the other.

But it is not enough to emphasize that the parables are theocentric, and that their primary concern is with faith in God. Faith in God needs definition. There is always the question of what God and what kind of faith. Such a qualification suggests that there is a further aspect of the parables that requires attention. It concerns the fact that their understanding of the theocentric was the object of the sharpest conflict. Jesus' opponents believed in God and readily agreed to the centrality of faith in him. Yet, their conception of what this involved differed so radically from his that the two were incompatible. The parables reflect this fact in the polemical spirit which pervades them. Although they are primarily concerned with faith in God, they are concerned with what it should mean over against the opponents' conception of it. Their choice of themes and characters, and the situations to which they are addressed, are colored by this purpose. One type of person is contrasted with another type: the prodigal with the elder brother, the tax collector with the Pharisee, the Samaritan with the priest and the Levite, the beggar with the rich man. In the tense atmosphere in which Jesus frequently conducted his ministry, the social and religious implications of these contrasts would be obvious. His opponents would get the point. In this respect, the parables peculiar to Luke, or most of them, have been rightly regarded as his controversial weapons against the critics and foes of his gospel.[2]

The issue was one that is best indicated by the crucial question: Does faith in God, as such, create the concern for the poor, the despised, and the outcast which characterized the ministry of Jesus? Does it create the concern which breaks through racial, national, and other distinctions to seek and save the lost? This question, which in a somewhat different form and setting confronts men today as they reflect upon the meaning of faith in God in relation to the human predicament, confronted Jesus. He was opposed by a form of faith which, instead of creating such concern, operated in various ways as a defense against it. Its counterpart in every period of history is a deity who tends to be represented as a symbol of refuge—a static, safe, introverted center into which men can escape from undesirable persons and circumstances, with faith regarded as a protective wall against corrupting influences. There is no outgoing, outreaching concern for the neighbor. There is no awareness of mission as an expression of love, no identification with the outsider. It makes men inquire whether out of a consciousness of love and a passion for justice it is not necessary to rid themselves of such a faith and free themselves of such a god.

The evidence indicates that Jesus had to break with such faith. He had to question it at the center. Consequently, he found himself involved in a conflict of such proportions that it eventually led to his crucifixion. Yet, through it all, as he sought the poor, the despised, and the outcast, the significance of his action was such that it virtually testified to his opponents: "You are wrong to reproach me for my intercourse with sinners as though it were godless behavior, for I am behaving toward sinners as God behaves; indeed, there is still more in it than this, for actually, God is acting through and in my action."[3]

II

The Elite or the Lost

(Luke 15:1–10)

Now the tax collectors and sinners were all drawing near to hear him. And the Pharisees and the scribes murmured, saying, "This man receives sinners and eats with them."

So he told them this parable: "What man of you, having a hundred sheep, if he has lost one of them, does not leave the ninety-nine in the wilderness, and go after the one which is lost, until he finds it? And when he has found it, he lays it on his shoulders, rejoicing. And when he comes home, he calls together his friends and his neighbors, saying to them, 'Rejoice with me, for I have found my sheep which was lost.' Even so, I tell you, there will be more joy in heaven over one sinner who repents than over ninety-nine righteous persons who need no repentance.

"Or what woman, having ten silver coins, if she loses one coin, does not light a lamp and sweep the house and seek diligently until she finds it? And when she has found it, she calls together her friends and neighbors, saying, 'Rejoice with me, for I have found the coin which I had lost.' Even so, I tell you, there is joy before the angels of God over one sinner who repents."

The critical attitude of the scribes and Pharisees who complained that Jesus received sinners and ate with them is a perennial one. It is the attitude which, from various sources, is responsible for the question being put to the church no less at the present time than in the ancient past:

14

Why this concern for sinners? Why this association with them? The presupposition which prompts the question is that what will strengthen and enhance the church is finding not the lost souls of the modern world but persons in a different category—popularly known as "the better people of the community." Whether in this instance the one category overlaps to any extent the other one is not the question—it is of course never asked—because the presupposition is that "the better people" constitute the best potential source of membership for the church. For the opinion is that no self-respecting Christian allows himself to become involved with persons of doubtful life and character. He always seeks the company of those whose influence is most desirable.

Whatever the form of the critical attitude to the evangelical, the reply Jesus gives is expressed in two of the most important and best-known of his parables—the lost sheep, and the lost coin. Each is phrased in the form of a question: "What man of you, having a hundred sheep, if he has lost one of them, does not leave the ninety-nine in the wilderness, and go after the one which is lost, until he finds it? . . . Or what woman, having ten silver coins, if she loses one coin, does not light a lamp and sweep the house and seek diligently until she finds it?"

These parables, which reflect the poverty of ancient Palestine, in which a single sheep was precious to a shepherd and the smallest coin to a housewife, will not be appreciated as much by modern people of prosperous circumstances. In most instances, the loss of a sheep is an experience they have never had. And if by chance they own a flock, it will probably be so large in this age of mass production that the loss of a single sheep would hardly be significant. The comfortable housewife will probably not even trouble to look for a lost coin. And should she find it, she will undoubtedly think it foolish to summon her neighbors to rejoice with her.

Had Jesus therefore chosen a more meaningful parable for such modern people, he might well have asked: "Which of you, if your child fails to return at night, do not contact the police and rush frantically about until search parties are organized and public announcements made, and the whole country is aroused to the fact that your child is lost? And when the child is found, which of you do not rejoice with your friends and neighbors and thousands of others that the lost is found?" The intensity with which a loving parent will search for his lost child and the joy he will experience on the child's recovery illustrate the point Jesus wished to make. It is the nature of God to seek the sinner with an ultimate concern and, upon his recovery, to rejoice with a corresponding joy. The lost sheep, the lost coin, the lost child—in fact, anything precious that is lost and that prompts a man to search for it with all the poignancy of an aching heart—speak of the love of God in his initiative for the rehabilitation of the sinner. The emphasis everywhere in the New Testament is upon this activity of God: sending, searching, coming, giving, pleading—centered in the ministry of Jesus, who in these parables defends his action against his critics.

It was this fact which the scribes and Pharisees failed to understand. They could not see why God should have such concern for the low, defiled, and subversive elements of society. The thought of his rejoicing as a parent over the return of thieves, beggars, and prostitutes seemed preposterous. His identification with them as exemplified by the conduct of Jesus, who received them and ate with them, seemed sacrilegious, for these were but the dregs of society, against whom the judgment of God should be pronounced. Why, therefore, be so rash as to represent

God as seeking after them, or heaven as a place jubilant over their return? Since they were responsible for their condition, why should the onus not be laid upon them to take the initiative and return? Let them prove their worthiness to be accepted of God and of his people, and then have joy in the satisfaction of their achievement. For why should the righteous run after sinners who in sinning resisted the thought of consulting the righteous? Why should the righteous attempt to make it easier for them and in so doing relieve the rigor of justice that the law requires and that sin by its nature merits?

It should be remembered, however, that the scribes and Pharisees included more persons under the category of sinners than those properly described as immoral. They included the broader category of the irreligious, who had less interest in the accumulated minutiae of religious observances and less ability to pay the Temple dues—such as tax collectors, shepherds, donkey drivers, tanners, peddlers, and, generally speaking, the peasant class. The term "sinners" had a social connotation, comparable in meaning to "outcasts," which went beyond the usual moralistic interpretation. Jesus' association with them was therefore more than a matter of keeping company with sinners in the strictly moral sense. It was a disregard of social status as religion presumed to define it. According to the custom of holding a teacher in highest esteem, this was a serious mark against him. For in addition to associating with the better people of the community (the religious) he was associating with the outcasts, who were at the bottom of the social scale (unholy). What place in the councils of the synagogues was there for donkey drivers and peddlers, and how could there be such joy in heaven over the return of one of these?[4]

What undoubtedly disturbed the scribes and Pharisees

was the specific character of the search for sinners. Had there been a way of seeking them which would have avoided an immediate contact—a way which from a distance or perhaps by proxy would have permitted the seeker to preserve his ceremonial sanctity—they would probably have welcomed it. Like those in favor of missions in strange and distant lands or in the downtown areas of disintegration in large cities but not at home, they were willing to accept missionary activity from a distance or by proxy. But the specific action of the shepherd who left the ninety-nine to seek the one lost sheep, and who on finding it laid it upon his shoulders and brought it back to the fold, forbade this possibility. His action was too particularized to admit any other conclusion than the one that obliged the religious to behave in a similar manner. It involved the same personal concern and tenderness exemplified by the prophetic figure of the shepherd gathering the lambs in his arms and carrying them in his bosom, and gently leading those with young. As applied to the sinner, it could only mean going to him, making personal contact with him, descending into the depths of his difficulty and even into his darkness, and finding him there.

Reluctance to engage in a search of this description is a perennial problem for the church. An inner resistance to the possibility of seeking the sinner is an obstacle that is always having to be overcome. The extent to which a general interest in missions, along with a similar general interest in church extension and promotion, may provide an escape from personal involvement is often surprising. Problems become of greater importance than persons, and loyalty to the church of greater importance than love to the individual, so that the general becomes a refuge from any obligation to that particular. What this means may be illustrated with a few minor adaptations from the experience a certain bewildered doctor once related of himself to the author of a famous novel. His perplexity was that the more he loved humanity in general, the less he could love man in particular. "In my dreams," he said, "I have often come to making enthusiastic schemes for the service of humanity . . . and yet I am incapable of living in the same room with anyone for two days together. . . . In twenty-four hours I hate the best of men: one because he is too long over his dinner, another because he has a cold and keeps blowing his nose. . . . But it has always happened that the more I detest men individually the more ardent becomes my love for humanity."[5]

The specific character of the search for sinners is the opposite of this. Its peculiar quality consists in the fact that it is able to do what this doctor found he could not do. It is able to live in close association with individuals without being irked by them—to bear with the man who is too long over his dinner and with the one who has a cold. It is able to accept the peculiarities of others and to love them just the same—even the peculiarities of the lost, which are its special task to find. As such, it characterized the ministry of Jesus, who did not come seeking humanity in general but man in particular—those whom he called by name as exemplified by his words to the tax collector Zacchaeus—words which when considered in the light of the divine initiative are all the more significant: "I must stay at your house today" (Luke 19:5).

It would be wrong, however, to conceive of the search for sinners as restricted to the socially inferior, as if instead of looking for better people, the task were that of looking for their opposites at the lower end of the social scale. The specific character of the search does not mean

the singling out of a special class either of the better or of
the poorer sort and concentrating the evangelical effort
on them. The one consideration is that the persons sought
are lost. That is to say, the qualifications of their sin as
"lostness" means that they are separated from God—
which applies as much to the better people as to the
poorer, to the religious as to the irreligious. Hence the
urgency of the fact that the shepherd leaves the ninety-
nine sheep to look for the one that is lost, and the woman
the nine coins to look for the one that is missing.

But in spite of the urgency and of the implicit recognition of "lostness" as the ultimate consequence of sin,
the parables do not focus upon it. They do not provide
the material for a study of lostness. They do not elaborate
it. They seem to take it for granted as the practical pre-
mise of their appeal—something so sufficiently understood and accepted that it need not be explained. To this
extent they contain a theme that not only is an important
aspect of the Biblical understanding of sin but is increasingly recognized in modern representations of the predicament of man, even though "sin" as a word is absent
from their vocabulary. As it relates to the common crowd
upon whom Jesus had compassion—to the tax collectors
and the peasants whom he received—it meant that they
wandered as sheep without a shepherd and were separated from the fold. As the victims of injustice who at
times repaid it with injustice, whose hard lot invited the
extreme, and whose indifference to formal religion involved the temptation to forget the God to whom it bore
such a questionable testimony, they were lost sheep in a
more serious respect than circumstances indicated. So,
frequently rejected by those who should have accepted
them, and subject to the wiles of demagogues, not surprisingly they sometimes felt that nothing mattered.

As we come now to the main focus of the parables, it must be said that in spite of the emphasis on the divine initiative, their attention is concentrated upon the joy there is in heaven over one sinner who repents. This is the evangelical refrain of the whole of the magnificent fifteenth chapter: "Rejoice with me, for I have found my sheep. . . . Rejoice with me, for I have found the coin which I had lost. . . . Let us eat and make merry; for this my son was dead, and is alive again; he was lost, and is found." In each instance the manner in which the response of the friends and neighbors is solicited suggests the exuberance of the heavenly joy. Moreover, the extent to which it is concentrated on the one repentant sinner is indicated by the sharp comparison: "There will be more joy in heaven over one sinner who repents than over ninety-nine righteous persons who need no repentance."

As such, it admits of no discrimination against the ninety-nine when understood in the context of love. For what the sinner receives is theirs to enjoy continually, which in the language of the father is familiarly expressed to the elder brother: "Son, you are always with me, and all that is mine is yours." The ninety-nine are therefore no more impoverished by the shepherd's leaving them behind to seek the one than the church is impoverished by its mission to the world. If heaven rejoices less over them than over the one, it is also true that when they are filled with love they rejoice less over themselves than over him.

The joy arises because the sinner is sought out of love. It is because he belongs to God as the sheep belongs to the shepherd and the coin to the woman that he is sought in such a manner. The thought of each as lost did not cause either the shepherd or the woman to disavow ownership—it did not cause them to become resigned to the circumstances and to say: "This sheep is no more mine. This coin is no more mine." Instead, it prompted them to assert their claim of ownership all the more strongly by engaging in a most persistent search. It only deepened their awareness of the preciousness of the property that was lost. In other words, the "lostness" did not nullify the basic "belongingness." This is Jesus' understanding of the relation of God to the sinner. The sinfulness of the sinner does not nullify the basic "belongingness" that binds him to God. It does not nullify the faithfulness of God as represented in the maintenance of a covenant relationship with him. Though the sinner lets go of God, God does not let go of him. Where sin increases, grace abounds all the more. (Rom. 5:20.)

The emphasis that Jesus puts upon the joyful reception of the sinner is directed particularly to the religious critics of his mission. These, whether ancient or modern, refuse to accept the sinner no matter how much he repents, or they accept him reluctantly and always with some degree of suspicion. In such a role the critics are probably less representative of a specific body of people than of the impulses that often emerge from the hearts of the most devout. For it has been ever thus. To experience difficulty in accepting a man who has been a notorious sinner is human. To experience the joy of heaven over him is the exception rather than the rule.

The problem appears in so many forms and enters so deeply into life that it is not difficult to illustrate. From the Biblical scene, the attitude of the Pharisee to the repentant tax collector in the Temple and the elder brother to the prodigal are the most familiar examples. From the modern scene, the reluctance of the religious to accept the repentant alcoholic, the converted criminal, the transformed atheist, and other similar problem-types is commonly recognized as one of the serious obstacles to their rehabilitation. The indifference manifested toward those persons experiencing grievous problems of the mind and spirit, out of which a living faith is emerging, is equally familiar. The joy which under these circumstances ought to be experienced by those persons whose privilege it is to receive the repentant and be identified with him is impaired by a strange resistance. This is not infrequently associated with a desire on the part of the religious to keep themselves and the body to which they belong pure within, or at least to preserve a recognizable social status —so much so that the repentant sinner is never allowed to forget that he has sinned. Since this tends to repel all but those who repent only of sin in general, and who apparently have no serious sin upon their conscience, it has the effect of restricting admissions to the better sort. As a consequence, the impression grows that repentance is not enough and indeed that Christ is not enough. For to both must be added the accumulated minutiae of conventional piety and social status that are the modern equivalents of the ancient tradition of the Pharisees.

A variation of the same problem occurs when the sinner is sought less out of love than out of the fact that he is a sinner. This lack of love is equivalent to another, subtler form of the same resistance that was previously recognized as open indifference. In this case, the seeker is highly conscious of the sinner's sin. He seeks the sinner primarily because of his lostness. This lostness is ever before him during the whole course of the seeking as the one obstacle that must be overcome. The intervening gulf of separation must be bridged. But when the sinner is won and the richest opportunity of fellowship and rehabilitation follows, the seeking stops. The seeker suddenly loses interest in him as if, with the obstacle overcome, there is little more to be done. There is no follow-up to the finding. Instead, the finding is itself the goal, which as a form of proselytism exemplifies the Shakespearean observation that all things that are, are with more spirit chased than enjoyed.[6]

When, however, the sinner is sought out of love, this sudden loss of interest does not occur. The seeking does not stop with the sinner's repentance. Instead, it continues. The same love that sought him as a lost man now seeks him as a rescued man. The dynamic of evangelism (*kērygma*) now becomes the dynamic of fellowship (*koinōnia*), because the two are in continuity with each other. So the seeking continues, as it is the nature of genuine love (*agapē*) always to do. But now it is unobstructed by the separation of lostness and by the resistance to it. It continues in the enjoyment of the fellowship and of the mutual enrichment of knowledge and experience in the service of the same Lord and Savior.

III

Beyond Religion and Irreligion
(Luke 15:11–32)

And he said, "There was a man who had two sons; and the younger of them said to his father, 'Father, give me the share of property that falls to me.' And he divided his living between them. Not many days later, the younger son gathered all he had and took his journey into a far country, and there he squandered his property in loose living. And when he had spent everything, a great famine arose in that country, and he began to be in want. So he went and joined himself to one of the citizens of that country, who sent him into his fields to feed swine. And he would gladly have fed on the pods that the swine ate; and no one gave him anything. But when he came to himself he said, 'How many of my father's hired servants have bread enough and to spare, but I perish here with hunger! I will arise and go to my father, and I will say to him, "Father, I have sinned against heaven and before you; I am no longer worthy to be called your son; treat me as one of your hired servants."' And he arose and came to his father. But while he was yet at a distance, his father saw him and had compassion, and ran and embraced him and kissed him. And the son said to him, 'Father, I have sinned against heaven and before you; I am no longer worthy to be called your son.' But the father said to his servants, 'Bring quickly the best robe, and put it on him; and put a ring on his hand, and shoes on his feet; and bring the fatted calf and kill it, and let us eat and make merry; for this my son was dead, and is alive again; he was lost, and is found.' And they began to make merry.

"Now his elder son was in the field; and as he came and drew near to the house, he heard music and dancing. And he called one of the servants and asked what this meant. And he said to him, 'Your brother has come, and your father has killed the fatted calf, because he has received him safe and sound.' But he was angry and refused to go in. His father came out and entreated him, but he answered his father, 'Lo, these many years I have served you, and I never disobeyed your command; yet you never gave me a kid, that I might make merry with my friends. But when this son of yours came, who has devoured your living with harlots, you killed for him the fatted calf!' And he said to him, 'Son, you are always with me, and all that is mine is yours. It was fitting to make merry and be glad, for this your brother was dead, and is alive; he was lost, and is found.'"

"There was a man who had two sons . . ." With these simple words the best-known of all the parables begins. The two sons, the one notorious in popular tradition as the prodigal, the other as his elder brother, are set before us. Each is representative of an element in first-century Jewish society. Each is symbolical—so that in their story is the story of two conflicting bodies of people, the one religious and the other irreligious. The story of these two is the story of similarly conflicting bodies in every society, and no less in modern society, where the conflict between the religious and the irreligious has assumed such proportions. But there is the father in the story, whose role is equally symbolical and who significantly enough has difficulty with both his sons. As the obvious symbol of deity, he has trouble with the religious as well as with the irreligious. So we are left to wonder in the end what advantage the one has over the other in coming to know and love him.

It was the younger son who took the initiative. He came

to his father and said, "Give me the share of property
that falls to me"—a demand that presupposed the Deu-
teronomic law of inheritance by which he was entitled
to a third of the estate and which, if his father desired,
could be apportioned during his lifetime (cf. Deut. 21:
17). The father at once responded. "He divided his living
between them." Whereupon the son with his share of the
estate in hand left his father behind and took his journey
into a distant land. In this he was doing only what
thousands of others have done who, on finding that the
eldest brother would inherit the landed portion of the
estate, have set out into the world to try their fortune.
Not infrequently a younger son has returned to his father's house in later years with a fortune. But in this
instance the opposite happened. The younger son was a
prodigal who knew neither the value of money nor the
importance of moral integrity. Having arrived in the far
country of his extravagant dreams, he wasted his substance in riotous living and soon spent all the money he
possessed. Like an irresponsible youth who for the first
time is out from under the discipline of his father and
who thinks of his new freedom only as an opportunity
for indulgence, he apparently yielded to his every desire.
Again, he was doing only what thousands of others have
done who in their reaction against the restraints of pa-
ternal law have misunderstood and misused their freedom once they have found it.

But this is more than the story of an ancient prodigal
or even of a modern prodigal, if we keep in mind the
symbolical function of the story. It represents the spiritual
problem exemplified both in the tax collectors and sinners
of Biblical times and in the irreligious of modern times
whose conception of freedom is equivalent to little more
than a desire to be independent of law. In principle, the

ancient scribes and Pharisees were right in their observation that the tax collectors and sinners—the latter more or less identical with the ignorant peasants—were lawless. No argument was required, of course, to convince them that the tax collectors were lawless, considering the manner in which they treated the average citizen. Little was required to convince them that the peasants were lawless, considering their negligence of the historic religious faith. Moreover, in the wider range of ancient society they were already convinced that the Gentiles were a people without the law.

In the modern situation the problem differs little from these various examples of its ancient counterpart. It is still a desire to be independent of law—a desire frequently concealed under a justifiable protest against the authoritarian image. Lawless freedom may be expressed in a variety of forms: the upthrust of dark, unrestrained psychical power; the onrush of wild revolutionary change; the unpredictable moods of the impressionist; and the less conspicuous but slothful spirit of the empty man whose life is lived from moment to moment and who is unaware of discipline or of destiny or of religious faith or fervor. The desire for lawless freedom is essentially a desire to be independent of the Father, who as deity is conceived under the category of law. In an attempt to wrest as much as possible out of life, to seize from nature all that human ingenuity and exploitation can grasp and in this manner to claim what it considers to be its inheritance, lawless freedom is but a colossal repetition of what the prodigal demanded. Accordingly, it takes its journey into the far country, which is aptly representative of the fact that freedom is conceived of as getting as far as possible away from God. This is presumably the one indispensable condition upon which it considers the enjoyment of its heritage possible.

If at this point we return to the story of the prodigal, we can see what happened to him as a consequence of his freedom. The Biblical text is highly descriptive. "And when he had spent everything, a great famine arose in that country, and he began to be in want. So he went and joined himself to one of the citizens of that country, who sent him into his fields to feed swine. And he would gladly have fed on the pods that the swine ate; and no one gave him anything." Put in the words of a common idiom, the freedom of the prodigal ended in the pigpen. It led to the place of hunger, poverty, degradation, and death. It brought him to the critical point where, though still a man, he was in danger of dying like a pig, far away, forgotten, and forsaken. Though still a son, he was lost as a consequence of a freedom that was really only a form of foolishness.

Again, the parallel obtains in the case of the prodigal's modern counterpart. As a consequence of irresponsible freedom, the predicament of the prodigal is repeated on a world-wide scale. In the desire to be independent of law, all law tends to be regarded as authoritarian and therefore to be resisted or revised at the whim of every pressure group. If it cannot be changed, the strategy is to disobey within the letter of the law or if the situation demands it, to stand upon the letter and appear more just than justice itself in order to advance the selfish interest. In these and other ways the spirit of modern man takes its journey into the far country away from God, whom it seems to conceive only under the category of law. To be without the law and beyond it, according to the ethos of the ancient Gentiles, seems to be the compelling idea of how to indulge in what has been appropriated from life and nature. The end result of such irresponsibility is inevitably a situation in which the ethics of the pigpen largely prevails and where humanity itself is endangered.

At this critical juncture in the story of the prodigal, an event occurred which, though outwardly unobservable, proved to be of the utmost importance in his life. "He came to himself." He saw where he had previously failed to see. He acquired insight into the pattern of conduct that had brought him to the lowest point of degradation. He recognized the falsity of his freedom and the necessity of retracing his steps as far as possible back to the place from which his tragic venture had begun—back to his father's house. His immediate problem was hunger. If he was to live, he had to eat. There was no time to lose. Like all men in the terrible privation of famine, it was only natural to think of the food available in his father's house, where even the lowest servants had bread enough and to spare. We must not cavil at the fact that as soon as he came to himself this was his first thought, even before the thought of confessing his sin and acknowledging his unworthiness to be called a son (vs. 17–19). Under similar circumstances the most spiritual-minded men would have thought and acted as he did. They too would have thought first of food. To attribute the realism of the starving prodigal to motives of expediency only detracts from the sincerity of the statement that he came to himself. Instead, we must recognize that he really had come to himself and was moved to penitence, so that the movement by which he returned to his father is best seen from beginning to end as possessing a unity. While he did not know as yet the magnanimity with which his father would welcome him, he knew enough to realize that something significant was beginning to happen in his life. So he arose and returned to his father.

For all he knew at this stage, his father might have rejected him and reacted in anger against his recklessness —which is a not infrequent reaction against a son who has wasted the best that his father has given him and has brought disgrace upon his home. But the father was an extraordinary father. One day while scanning the road in a wistful hope that his son would return, as any parent will do whose love is too deep and enduring to be shattered by the waywardness of one of his own, he suddenly recognized the prodigal a great way off. The delicate cue of familiar mannerisms known intuitively only to love revealed his identity. The filthy rags and the haggard appearance could not conceal from the father who he was. The father's response was instantly one of compassion, so that he ran to meet him, threw his arms around him, and kissed him—actions which spoke volumes of meaning, surpassing the best of language in communicating the response of one heart to another. In the high significance of such a moment, the parable represents the magnanimity of the grace of God as it encounters the guilty conscience of man. For before the prodigal could finish his confession, the initiative of his father's love had interrupted him. At once his father had servants bring forth the best robe and put it on him, and a ring on his finger and shoes on his feet—acts symbolical of the highest honor and status and of the unconditional manner in which he had been accepted. The robe distinguished him as a special guest, the ring signified authority, and the shoes showed that he was free and not slave. In order to crown these acts with appropriate joy and thanksgiving, the father ordered the fatted calf to be killed so that the whole household might celebrate the occasion with a bountiful feast. "Let us eat and make merry; for this my son was dead, and is alive again; he was lost, and is found."

Such an unconditional welcome of the prodigal represents the manner in which God accepts the sinner back into communion with him. It is the new and decisive consideration in the parable, which to be fully appreciated has to be seen in contrast to what the prodigal thought he deserved. He wanted to return, but only to the lowest place. He could not conceive of returning to his father without imposing a penalty on himself as a compensation for sin. His only thought was to demean himself to the lowest possible status—that of a hired servant who did not have even the security of a slave and who as a casual laborer could be dismissed without notice. Whether he hoped eventually to prove himself, or was obsessed only with the thought of punishing himself, is impossible to determine. But there is little doubt that he was burdened with a deep consciousness of guilt, as his preconceived confession with its forthright request for a demotion of status so clearly indicates: "Father, I have sinned against heaven and before you; I am no longer worthy to be called your son; treat me as one of your hired servants."

It is similar with the irreligious of the modern era, when out of awareness of the critical nature of the situation they come to themselves and wonder if there may not be something in religion after all. They return to it with the same understanding of God as the God of law from which they had formerly escaped. The only difference is that the direction is now reversed. Like the prodigal, they assume that certain conditions ought to be required that will limit them to an inferior role or compel them to prove themselves before being accepted fully into the fellowship of the church. They may prefer to remain on the periphery more or less as outsiders. If they move into the center, they may wish to compensate for wasted time and opportunity, in which case a surprising readiness to accept rules and formulas, traditions and practices, somewhat uncritically may be part of the self-punishing impulse to fulfill the demands of justice (conscience). Their return to religion is in this respect a return to law and to the God of law whom they assume the father represents—albeit the law as conceived out of the uneasiness of a remorseful conscience. Consequently, it is the greatest surprise for them to be confronted with the God of grace, whose magnanimity accepts them unconditionally and restores them at once to full status in the household of faith. It is the greatest surprise for them to meet him in the lives of others and to be accepted of them in his name in a similarly unconditional manner. It is a totally new experience—different from anything predictable on the basis of law, from which at first they desired to be independent and to which they would now return. They are really accepted with no further conditions to fulfill—which means that they have found the freedom which at first they thought they would find by leaving God behind for atheism. They are now lawless in a new sense, because they have found that the God to whom they have returned is "lawless" and in no sense authoritarian. His grace transcends the requirements of justice. As otherwise expressed, it requires more than justice to save man. The God whom they thought they knew is so different from what they expected that they can only inquire if in the first instance they knew him at all.

The latter part of the parable is devoted to the elder brother, whose attitude toward the prodigal affords such a sharp contrast with that of the father. The description of his reaction is graphic and dramatic: As he drew near the house and heard music and dancing he was greatly surprised and curious to know what they meant. When informed by one of the servants that his brother had come and that his father had killed the fatted calf to celebrate the occasion, his immediate reaction was anger. He refused to enter the house. He would have no part in the welcome. When his father came out and entreated him to enter, he was sharply critical. "Lo, these many years I have served you, and I never disobeyed your command; yet you never gave me [as much as] a kid, that I might make merry with my friends. But when this son of yours [not my brother] came, who has devoured your living with harlots, you killed for him the fatted calf."

The immediate impression—and the one that the elder brother believes and wishes to promote—is that the father is guilty of a grave injustice. The father is portrayed as a fickle parent easily influenced by a ne'er-do-well who after wasting his share of the estate on immoral women returns home to live off the rest of the family, who have worked faithfully and hard in the interval without the slightest luxury. The lavish welcome accorded such a character is interpreted as the rankest favoritism, involving an almost total disregard of justice. What makes the situation worse and acutely offensive is that he is to be allowed to live off the portion of the estate that rightfully belongs to his elder brother. Moreover, the father, by the act of putting a ring on his finger, has given him authority. No wonder the elder brother is angry.

It was doubtless the intention of Jesus to emphasize this offensive feature of the story and to indicate by means of it how the grace of God is always offensive to those who insist on justice and nothing more. It is the same

offensive feature made explicit in the parable of the workmen who bore the burden and heat of the day only to
discover at the end that they received the same as those
who had labored only an hour. Religious people everywhere tend to react in a similar manner to the thought
that long years of service in the life and work of the
church does not put them in a position in relation to God
essentially different from that of a disreputable character
off the street who like the thief on the cross decides to
repent at the last minute. They complain—and sometimes
bitterly—that there is something decidedly unfair about
the gospel. For it seems to give the irreligious an advantage over the religious, in view of which the tempting
question emerges: Why not sin that grace may abound?
(Rom. 6:1). Why not live irreligiously all one's life without concern for church life and work, and repent only at
the end and receive the lavish welcome of a prodigal?

The problem confronting us here is the certainty with
which the religious believe they are competent to judge
right and wrong and to assess their status before Almighty
God. The trouble lies in the facility with which the elder
brother feels he can judge the father. It lies in the ease
with which the religious presume to judge not only themselves and the irreligious but God himself, who in his
mysterious creative power is the author and sustainer of
their very existence. There is justice. But there is also a
calculative spirit, which can operate under the canopy of
justice. Such a spirit has its catalog of rules all too easily
defined and applied. It has little appreciation of the depth,
complexity, and mystery of genuine justice. It knows
exactly what is right and wrong, as it knows that two and
two make four. But for this reason it fails to understand
that the whole fabric of such knowledge is inextricably
interwoven with the prevailing ideology. Like the old

wine-skin bottles of the parable, it has to be shattered by the expansive power of the new wine, which is symbolical of the grace of God. In other words, the gospel is not an additional power, message, or insight that completes the fabric of little rules within which the individual feels secure—that fabric which convinces him of his competency to judge. Instead, the gospel is a disturbing event involving a radical readjustment of what he understands by right and wrong. In other words, the hearing of the gospel introduces into his life the new justice, which shatters the old. It was to those who were confident of their ability to assess their status before God that Jesus said, "When you have done all that is commanded you, say, 'We are unworthy servants; we have only done what was our duty'" (Luke 17:10).

The elder brother, like those whose long record of service in religious work leads them to look askance at a disreputable character off the street who has only of late entered into the joy of salvation, was completely convinced that he was a profitable servant. He was so enslaved by the old facile ideas of what was right and wrong that he was unable to see the new and higher justice in the welcome his father gave the prodigal and why he as the elder brother should have participated in it. To him the new and higher justice was completely wrong. The only right way was the old calculative justice which ultimately asks, How much is there in it for me? It was this same conception of justice which moved Peter to ask of Jesus: "Lo, we have left everything and followed you. What then shall we have?" It moved the mother of the sons of Zebedee to seek for her two sons prominent positions in the Messianic Kingdom, the one son on the right hand of Christ and the other on the left. In this way, under the canopy of justice men promote their selfish

interests, especially in those situations where justice seems
to favor them and where it can be exploited to the utmost.
They have no profound concern or love toward those less
fortunate who may be better served were they not to press
so ardently for justice.

But no matter how just the elder brother's claim may
appear to be, its plausibility is in doubt because of the
complex of anger that motivated it. It does not possess
the clear and balanced perspective of righteous anger,
typical of a prophetic protest, but is deeply distorted by
personal references. Although the inheritor of the whole
of the landed estate, he dares to accuse his father of
never giving him as much as a kid. Although in comparison with what his prodigal brother had originally received he was much the richer, with the prodigal now
reduced to beggardom he was incomparably richer. As
one whose favorable situation could be described in the
words of the father—"Son, you are always with me, and
all that is mine is yours"—he could only complain how
badly he was treated. He would not deign even to recognize his brother. He hated him. The chasm of separation
between them, as indicated by his accusation, scorn, sar-
casm, and hardness of heart, was to all intents and purposes unbridgeable. The same chasm separated him from
his father, from whom he seemed to be as far away and as
alienated as the prodigal ever was in the distant land of
his reckless quest for freedom. The error of the elder
brother was that he assumed no responsibility for the
prodigal. If the latter wasted his money, sank into sin
and misery, and was lost forever, it was nothing to him.
If he repented and tried to find his way back into his
home and into society, that was nothing to him. In no
respect did the elder brother consider himself his brother's
keeper. Yet he pleaded the justice of his position—the

justice of maintaining his share of the estate free from any obligation to his brother. But in doing so—in all his insistence upon justice—the one question that must always be put to him and to those whom in every age he represents is: How can a man who has no ultimate concern for others really know what justice is? How can he be serious about justice without recognizing that it is precisely in such a concern for others that genuine justice is to be found and that, in the case of the parable, the magnanimity of the father was exemplified?

It is obvious that the portrait of the elder brother represents the reaction of the scribes and Pharisees against the magnanimity of Jesus in his reception of the irreligious tax collectors and peasants. He had received them in the same spirit in which the father in the parable had received the prodigal. But like the father, who soon discovered how his action had provoked the anger of the elder son, Jesus soon discovered how his action had provoked the anger of the scribes and Pharisees. In his compassionate acceptance of the irreligious he had provoked the wrath of the religious. The fact that this should happen is no surprise when it is remembered how sharply divided the Pharisees were from the peasants, in what almost amounted to a castelike separation. A Pharisee, for instance, would never allow himself to become the guest of a peasant. He would never entertain one in his home without due precaution. He would not sell him any product of the field, or visit him, or travel with him, or allow his daughter to marry him.[7] Jesus' reception of such people was therefore more than a rebuke to the self-righteousness of the scribes and Pharisees considered as a subjective quality. It was a rebuke to the self-justification by which a way of life maintains itself and commands the obedience of its devotees without their realizing how socially discriminating it is.

It is the calculative spirit of this wider self-justification as it pervades established religion that is represented by the elder brother. His is the self-congratulatory attitude of such religion on never having escaped from God into the far country of immoral men, secularists, or atheists. It is also the secret satisfaction of witnessing to any extent the failure of the prodigals and, especially, their slow, trudging homeward journey back to faith. But whoever the prodigals may be, such religion by its judgmental attitude closes the door against them. Its piety repels them. Although they may be genuinely dissatisfied with their lot and sincerely moved to return to God, its calculative spirit in all it does and plans and evaluates, in its conception of God and of his will, in its view of man and of the world and even of destiny, is a measure of its inability to accept and welcome them. It is a measure of its failure to love them. And since, moreover, there is no hint of the elder brother's ever being reconciled to the father and to the prodigal, the suggestion will remain that such failure as a form of opposition to the graciousness of God within religion is more dangerous than the escape from God into irreligion. At least the latter in its nakedness may be seen for what it is, while the former remains concealed.

IV

The Crisis of Love

(Luke 10:25–37)

And behold, a lawyer stood up to put him to the test, saying, "Teacher, what shall I do to inherit eternal life?" He said to him, "What is written in the law? How do you read?" And he answered, "You shall love the Lord your God with all your heart, and with all your soul, and with all your strength, and with all your mind; and your neighbor as yourself." And he said to him, "You have answered right; do this, and you will live."

But he, desiring to justify himself, said to Jesus, "And who is my neighbor?" Jesus replied, "A man was going down from Jerusalem to Jericho, and he fell among robbers, who stripped him and beat him, and departed, leaving him half-dead. Now by chance a priest was going down that road; and when he saw him he passed by on the other side. So likewise a Levite, when he came to the place and saw him, passed by on the other side. But a Samaritan, as he journeyed, came to where he was; and when he saw him, he had compassion, and went to him and bound up his wounds, pouring on oil and wine; then he set him on his own beast and brought him to an inn, and took care of him. And the next day he took out two denarii and gave them to the innkeeper, saying, 'Take care of him; and whatever more you spend, I will repay you when I come back.' Which of these three, do you think, proved neighbor to the man who fell among the robbers?" He said, "The one who showed mercy on him." And Jesus said to him, "Go and do likewise."

This expert in the sacred law of Israel who was intent upon putting Jesus to the test knew what question would lead most directly into the center of religious life and thought: "What shall I do to inherit eternal life?" As the question of questions that would at once reveal the breadth and depth of a teacher's understanding of the answer to human destiny and therefore of the fundamental concern of Biblical testimony, it was unsurpassed. But he also knew the answer to give as Jesus turned the question back upon him, for his summary statement of the essence of the law was also unsurpassed in excellence. "You shall love the Lord your God with all your heart, and with all your soul, and with all your strength, and with all your mind; and your neighbor as yourself." Eternal life is to be found in the realization of love toward God, the neighbor, and oneself—with the love of God as normative and at the same time indicative of a total commitment to him. In other words, such love is the answer to the ultimate problem of human existence, which in modern times is frequently known as the "problem of God." The lawyer (scribe) was undoubtedly an able theologian.

As with any penetrating theological exchange in which the participants are thoroughly conversant with Scripture and relevant subject matter, it is one thing to state the truth in the form of questions and answers but another to transform it into life and action. The gulf between theory and practice is always the stumbling block. "Do this, and you will live" will always create embarrassment and possibly provoke a crisis at the secret center of a man's life if he takes the imperative seriously. The simple command to "do it" will be enough to shake the foundations of any theological superstructure. In the present instance, apart from other motives that undoubtedly entered into the mind of the scribe, this was probably the reason why he sought to justify himself and why, like most people under similar embarrassment, he attempted to do so by asking another question: "Who is my neighbor?" It was not so much that he was crafty and wished to outwit this strange teacher whom he had chosen to test, but that he was posing a question which in different ways was exercising the conscience of scores of his compatriots. It was a basic question, which from the nature of their faith had emerged at the practical level as one that was probably often discussed and that now, in serious theological exchange, was the logical one to ask.

The reason for this will be better appreciated by recognizing the probability that the scribe would be either identified with the Pharisees or associated with them. As a leader of those persons who conceived of their scrupulous dedication to holiness as the hope of their nation and the hope of the individual, he would be actuated by a desire to separate himself from all things common or unclean. The emphasis on separatism would undoubtedly accentuate the question of the identity of the neighbor. For it must be remembered how carefully the Pharisees avoided the irreligious, whose neglect of the sacred law had presumably rendered them potential sources of defilement. Where to draw the line was always the practical question and frequently the difficult one. Within the fellowship of the Pharisees themselves, there was of course less if any difficulty, because by definition they were all neighbors together—as their self-selected name "associates" (*haberim*) suggests. But the problem was in defining the circle in which their fellowship was circumscribed.

Their conception of holiness was no different in principle from the self-righteousness of any self-encircled group that equates its neighbors with those on the inside. Since their fellowship was turned in upon itself in the conviction of a unique power or quality (meritoriousness) at its disposal, their attitude to the outsider was generally negative. Their fellowship was not open to him. It had no readiness for him. They could not seek and love and accept him as he was, but only as he fulfilled the conditions defined by what their fellowship was and presumed to possess.

But even when holiness is not conditioned in such a manner by self-righteousness, it raises the question of the identity of the neighbor because it involves a unique principle of separation. To be holy is to be separate. It is to be set apart unto the Lord. This primary meaning reveals a difference that comes between one man and another and compels them to ask in what respect they now are neighbors. The problem arises because the identification with others that love involves as a condition of neighborliness is limited by the separation implicit in holiness. At this point there are two dangerous temptations. One temptation, which we have already seen in the case of the Pharisees and of all self-encircled religious groups, is to find the neighbor only within the restricted area defined by the conception of holiness. The other temptation which is a reaction to the first, is to eliminate all holiness (transcendence) and lapse into a love that is but a pantheistic identification with humanity or a section of it, in which all are neighbors. It will be evident, therefore, how important it is to have an adequate understanding of holiness and of the tension that always exists between it and love. On this understanding will depend how the identity of the neighbor is established. The question of whether holiness separates a man from others or unto them, whether it turns him inward upon himself or outward to them, will be decisive.

In a larger perspective, the question is of relevance both to Israel and to the church in their understanding of themselves as elect people who are therefore distinguished and separated from the world. Election by its nature creates the problem of the neighbor in a unique and unavoidable form. Consequently, it is a highly representative problem—the kind that in different ways, but ultimately for the same reason, both Jews and Christians sooner or later will always consider. It is really their question par excellence, which defines for them at the point of interrogation a common ground. Within this common ground, as each group asks it of the other, it reaches a height of seriousness that is probably found in no other comparable exchange between two religions.

The scribe whose expert knowledge of the sacred law would therefore make him sensitive to this problem, illustrates the kind of dilemma that always tends to arise out of it. For at the same time that he advocated the love of God and neighbor, he was in serious doubt as to the identity of his neighbor. Although urging the necessity of love, he did not know the object of love. From his point of view, the answer to the dilemma seems to have been for the most part relatively simple, because the form of his question implies that a definition of the object of love is an answer to the problem of love. But since there is reason to doubt the validity of this assumption, is it legitimate to ask whether the difficulty in defining the identity of his neighbor was more subjective than objective and therefore a product of having failed to love? Or was it even more than this? Perhaps it was failure to love God, with a consequent failure to love his neighbor, as would be suggested by the association of the two deficiencies in the First Letter of John: "He who does not love his brother whom he has seen, cannot love God whom he has not seen" (I John 4:20).

But Jesus did not provide the scribe with an answer that would allow him to find refuge in the abstract or to lose himself in the complications of casuistry. He told him a story that was so vivid and dramatic in form and of such a degree of probability that it was the same as looking at everyday life. The scene was the lonely road that traversed the barren, uninhabited, precipitous region between Jerusalem and Jericho. The road was notorious for robbery and violence, and probably as familiar to the scribe as the place where he lived. As an illustration of existing social conditions there would be little that was hypothetical about it, particularly to those who traveled. "A man was going down from Jerusalem to Jericho, and he fell among robbers, who stripped him and beat him, and departed, leaving him half-dead." The incident could not be mistaken for anything other than it was: violence against the innocent, man in his brutality to man, a criminal emergency. It was one of those critical situations of everyday life better known to police, hospital attendants, and social workers than to the incumbents of book-filled studies and candled sanctuaries. It cried out for action—for something to be done, and done quickly—and an interruption of normal pursuits because of the urgent necessity of saving a life. The immediate obligation involved a rolling up of the sleeves and a soiling of the hands capable of revealing the identity of the neighbor.

Significantly enough, the first two travelers to appear on the scene were representatives of organized religion—the one a priest, the other a Levite, who, as the story indicates, came that way by chance. Both men were associ-

ated with the magnificent Temple at Jerusalem, which for
its architectural grandeur would qualify as one of the
wonders of the Middle East, and because of its wealth,
power, and influence was undoubtedly the center of ancient Jewry. Both men were associated with the ministry
of God. The priest could claim charismatic power, the
knowledge of liturgy and law, and an ordained status in
the holy succession of those set apart to the priestly office.
The Levite was devoted to lesser tasks of a practical nature, who in the role of an assistant would always be a
right-hand man. When they arrived, what did they do?
How did they react to what they saw? As religious men
who found themselves confronted by criminal injustice
and critical human need, of what practical relevance was
their religion? The strange, inescapable answer is that
their religion permitted them to get around the wounded,
helpless, half-dead victim on the road. Each kept on the
opposite side and passed him by. With no sign of concern
or feeling for the misfortune of another, each left him behind to die. To this extent, the priest and the Levite, for all
their religion, were no better than the thieves and ban-
dits who had already abandoned him.

It is idle to plead that the priest and the Levite were
victims of an unfortunate system and on this account to
play down the gravity of their conduct. It is as idle as to
plead—and this perhaps on better grounds—that the robbers were victims of an unfortunate system, for the one
plea is as valid as the other. Neither plea modifies the
lovelessness to which the victim on the road was a mute
but tragic testimony. The obvious inference is that the
priest and the Levite exhibited a callousness that by any
elemental standard of decency, ancient or modern, was
devoid of social conscience. If there is any mistaken tendency to condemn them by the norms of enlightened hu-

manitarianism, the ethical witness of their own law and prophets will be severe enough. In this respect, they were probably more representative of the manner in which religion in any place or period may become insensitive to shock and evade its responsibility for social justice and rehabilitation in situations involving man's inhumanity to man than we ordinarily appreciate. The priestly class in Palestine were never known to have championed the cause of the oppressed people of the land (peasants) under Herodian and Roman rule.

But why did the priest and the Levite pass by on the other side? This question deserves attention even though its answer is not provided in the text and is suggested only by the probabilities of the religious situation of the time. First, the wounded man was probably a source of religious defilement. For all they knew, he could have been dead, or an irreligious man such as a peasant or a tax collector, or even a man without the law—a Gentile. According to the tradition, contact with such would have defiled them and made it necessary to observe the appropriate ceremonies for the restoration of purity. The fear of defilement would be strong enough to prevent the emergence of any feeling of pity for the victim. There would be even less pity if the fear was re-enforced by the conviction that his misfortune was a sign of the judgment of God. On this basis, it would be easy and indeed necessary to pass by on the opposite side, not only for the preservation of holiness, but to avoid a presumptuous interference with the operation of judgment. It would be especially presumptuous if the victim was considered to be under a curse, for in this case, to help the man would incur the risk of becoming involved in the curse.

The second probability was the risk of incurring legal responsibility. In both ancient and modern times, with various differences from one country to the other but always with a surprising degree of consistency, the rendering of assistance can easily involve the would-be helper in legal entanglements. Under certain conditions, to the astonishment of the innocent interpreter of the parable anxious to apply it to everyday life, he finds himself in more difficulty than he bargained for. Without suspecting it, he may have become the victim's legal guardian and involved himself in financial liability. The law, both in its ancient and modern forms, may so ensnare the sincere good neighbor anxious to lend his help that some legal experts advise that it is generally wise to pass by on the other side. If this fact seems to discourage neighborliness, it is stated only to suggest the risk that is always involved in really seeking to help another. If, as already conjectured, the law of holiness restrained the priest and the Levite from rendering assistance, it should be remembered that there is a sense in which all law restrains such assistance. That is to say, when love becomes radical enough to break through the accepted rules of society in an expression of ultimate concern for others, it not infrequently encounters the law. This fact the ministry of Jesus clearly indicates.

The crucial figure in the parable—and the one that elicits the greatest surprise—is the Samaritan. The selection of him to exemplify the meaning of love to a neighbor and therefore to indicate indirectly the answer to the original question would be offensive to the scribe. It would be as offensive as the selection of a member of a despised race or political party to a respectable but narrowly sensitive nationalist in the modern world. For the Samaritans were a people with whom the Jews had no dealings. They were a mongrel breed, considered to be a source of spiritual defilement, and their land was avoided by pious Jews on journeys to and from Galilee. They were not permitted in the Jewish Temple. The testimony of a Samaritan was not acceptable in a Jewish court of law. Daily in the synagogues prayers were offered for the denial of their salvation. Yet it was one of these people whom Jesus chose as the chief figure in the parable to exemplify the highest form of love—and this to a Jewish theologian. The selection could hardly be more offensive. Yet it illustrated in an amazing way those familiar words of Paul: "God chose what is foolish in the world to shame the wise, . . . what is low and despised in the world . . . to bring to nothing things that are, so that no human being might boast in the presence of God (I Cor. 1:27–29). The answer to the original question was to come from a most unexpected source—from the enemy, as it were. It was suggestive of how our neighbor may identify himself to us out of those who, humanly speaking, are often against us, and thus it suggested that we have no monopoly on the divine presence.

The immediate reaction of the Samaritan to the unfortunate man was to have compassion on him. This suggests the personal feeling indicated by the familiar modern expression "to have a heart." His compassion was the source of all the beneficent conduct that followed, including his deep identification with the man's tragic plight—an immediate response with no proud precaution of first trying to ascertain his worthiness. There is no evidence of the Samaritan's inquiring whether the man was a Jew, or about his status, his ancestry, his religion, or his political affiliation. The compassion of his heart immediately bridged the gap without recourse to such knowledge. He at once recognized the urgency of the moment—the need for quick, decisive action.

His next reaction was to respond to the man's need in the most practical and sensible manner. He did not merely stand gazing, in a prolonged indulgence of his feelings as though the man could be helped by sympathy alone. He acted. He went to him and bound up his wounds, pouring in oil and wine—two of the commonest forms of ancient medication. There was no fear on his part of spiritual defilement, no concern over the possible compromising of his holiness, and if there was the risk of legal responsibility, he apparently accepted it.

But his love for the unfortunate man did not stop with the rendering of aid at the scene of the crime. It had an eye to the future. It had the persistence of a concern that saw the man through his trouble to the end. Consequently, we find that the Samaritan interrupted his travel schedule by putting the man on his own beast and bringing him to an inn. It is evident that he did not merely serve up to the point where it interfered with self-interest and where so many say: "That is all we can do. We have to go. This man has already taken enough of our time." Instead, he made provision for him to be sheltered, fed, and cared for until his recovery from his unfortunate experience, and as a sign of concern even remained in the inn overnight himself. The generous nature of such provision is clearly stated in the familiar words: "And the next day he took out two denarii and gave them to the innkeeper, saying, 'Take care of him; and whatever more you spend, I will repay you when I come back.' "

In such a spontaneous expression of love and concern which exemplified the quality of the unconditional we have more than ordinary goodness, more than ordinary charity. This conclusion increasingly commends itself as we reflect on the crescendo of the Samaritan's conduct from his first reaction of compassion until his final provision of monetary assistance. His action represents much more than humanitarianism. It is much more than charity.

It is that radical love so often emphasized in the New Testament in various kinds of incidents and responses and in the teaching of Jesus. It is ever related, however secretly and indirectly, to the grace of God exemplified in Jesus' own life and mission. In this respect it is the ethic of grace. If this be not appreciated, any doubt of its extraordinary character will be dispelled by reflecting upon the rarity with which the best of us will provide a complete stranger, under similarly tragic circumstances, with what amounts in modern terminology to an open account.

But Jesus did not leave the question concerning the neighbor suspended in mid-air. At the conclusion of the parable he turned to the scribe and asked, "Which of these three, do you think, proved neighbor to the man who fell among the robbers?" And the scribe replied without hesitation, "The one who showed mercy on him." At this point, the academic observation that such an answer does not correspond to the original question is of little significance in the light of the complexity of the problem of love, which is pastoral in its connotation. The bare fact that the scribe inquired about the object of love is no reason for concluding that the real answer to his query will be given in these terms. Jesus' question at the end of the parable concerned the subject of such love: Who acted as neighbor? The fact that he understood it, not as a theoretical problem to be kept always in the objective context as the theologians are wont to do, but as a personal problem, the answer to which is necessarily subjective, is confirmed by his final injunction: "Go and do likewise." Thus, the objective question, "Who is my neighbor?" is answered by the recognition that if one acts like a neighbor, one will discover who his neighbor is. Real love never asks who is to be its object, because this implies a conditional approach, a consciousness of the possibility of either giving or withholding itself. Instead, it gives unconditionally and with a strange spontaneity and indiscrimination which by its nature always discovers the object because of its ability to break through the lines of color, class, and creed.

Such an answer is at the same time suggestive of the answer to the deeper question of faith in God. Had the scribe inquired, "Who is my God?" the answer would probably have been no different in principle from what the parable provides, because the two questions are interrelated. The same giving of the self that is sharply contrasted with the withholding of the self involved in objectivity would have enabled him to find the answer to his question as he presumably did to the other. Since the God of the Bible is characterized as one who identifies himself with the victims of injustice to the extent of going down into the depths of human misery and suffering and taking the burden upon his heart, we can assume the same identification in the case of the wounded, half-dead man on the road to Jericho. Passing him by on the other side is tantamount to passing the God of the Bible by on the other side. It is tantamount to an evasion of the divine imperative arising out of the situation as its implicitly spiritual qualification. The same is true of all forms of indifference to the victims of man's inhumanity to man—ancient or modern. Hardness of heart, insensitivity to suffering, the inability to be shocked, the silent treatment, and the generally depersonalized character of modern life are all indicative of an evasion of the divine imperative. It is more than a question of literally circumventing a victim on the road. The road is everyday life. The indifference is a sign of the real godlessness of the day, whether of the religious or of the irreligious.

But the hortatory function of the parable is not restricted to the imperative of responding as the Samaritan

did and of renouncing the indifference of the priest and
the Levite, in whose conduct we detect ourselves and our
introverted pattern of life and religion. It includes the
representative role of the victim, whose predicament reveals our situation in so far as misfortune and injustice
have overtaken us and left us lying naked and beaten and
half dead along the road of everyday life. There we may
lie with only the faintest if any effective hope of the existence of the God of grace who would move into the
situation and render unconditional aid by means of strange
Samaritan hands. The indifference which in other directions has concealed from us the deepest need of our
brother may conceal from us the love from which nothing
can separate us (Rom. 8:38–39). Therefore, every figure in
the parable—the victim lying bleeding by the side of the
road, the indifferent priest and Levite who passed by on
the other side, the good Samaritan who showed compassion—reveals to us ourselves in relation to others and to
the God of grace to whom we belong. The first figure reveals our need of him, the second our religious resistance
to him, and the third the neighborliness by means of
which through us God would reveal his love to the broken
and bruised, the hopeless and abandoned, along the road
of life.

V

The Insider and the Outsider
(Luke 18:10–14)

"Two men went up into the temple to pray, one a Pharisee and the other a tax collector. The Pharisee stood and prayed thus with himself, 'God, I thank thee that I am not like other men, extortioners, unjust, adulterers, or even like this tax collector. I fast twice a week, I give tithes of all that I get.' But the tax collector, standing far off, would not even lift up his eyes to heaven, but beat his breast, saying, 'God, be merciful to me a sinner!' I tell you, this man went down to his house justified rather than the other; for every one who exalts himself will be humbled, but he who humbles himself will be exalted."

Who were these men? What does it mean that one was a Pharisee and the other a tax collector? Is it enough to know that one was religious, the other irreligious; one inordinately conscious of his holiness, the other despairingly aware of his sinfulness? Is it enough to know that one was so punctilious in his observance of the sacred law that a sharp line of castelike separation divided him from the other, a presumably low, degraded outcast? Is it enough to know that one was highly patriotic, whereas the other, as the agent of a foreign power, exerted a subversive influence and was hated by the average citizen? If we know them to this extent—one deeply devoted to holiness, the other of a hardened underworld mentality—

we will be surprised that in the parable two men of such opposite character would be going up into the Temple to pray. For the Pharisee, it would not be other than a customary act upon which he would undoubtedly lay much emphasis both because of the example it would set for others and because of the necessity of fostering holiness to resist the tide of worldliness. But for the tax collector, it would be an unusual act, because he was not of the type that frequented the Temple. His presence in the Temple, and more especially at prayer, would be in fact anomalous.

Not unexpectedly, therefore, considering such contrasted habits of spirituality, their prayers were as opposite in character as they themselves. "The Pharisee stood and prayed thus with himself, 'God, I thank thee that I am not like other men, extortioners, unjust, adulterers, or even like this tax collector. I fast twice a week, I give tithes of all that I get.' " Although addressed to God, it is a prayer of a man who is thankful not for divine mercy but for the fact that his piety distinguished him from the rest of men and placed him in a class by himself. Conscious of the separation his holiness has introduced between himself and others, and the freedom from sin it has presumably conferred upon him, he is not only grateful for his piety but convinced of his salvation. Judged from the fact that he confessed no sin, it would appear that he had no appreciable consciousness of sin. From an immediate point of view, however, his prayer was characterized by a sickening egotism. Its fivefold use of the first person singular is made quite unashamedly in no less a place than the Temple itself, where a more appropriate response from a Jew loyal to the prophetic faith would have given God the glory. With a confidence that revolved so completely around himself in the presence of God and that betrayed the secret center of his ultimate security, it is doubtful whether he really believed in God.

This suggests that it would be a mistake to regard his attitude as only that of egotism in its usual connotation. For goodness is here becoming conscious of itself as goodness over against God and therefore independent of him. Sin is manifesting itself under the category of goodness, which is the characteristic subtlety of all legalism. The Pharisee is good and he knows it, and in the knowledge of it his goodness is vitiated. As always happens in the human heart at the height of noble achievement, the awareness of goodness becomes the worm that devours it from within. Aware of it himself, man desires that others be aware—that even heaven itself should know, and in such knowledge accept the claim it imposes on divine recognition and favor. The prayer of the Pharisee is always popular, despite the things said against it in sober moments. It is popular because his piety strikes a common chord with those who, though not of such spiritual diligence, admire him for his sincerity. As the prayer of man's self-justification before God, it echoes the philosophy of success in things religious, ancient or modern, to the right or to the left. To regard his prayer as exceptional is to ignore one of the deepest and commonest problems of contemporary spiritual life. For it is evident that we insist on acting like the Pharisee, building our lives upon his presuppositions. When the critical moment comes, we fight with all our resources to defend what his prayer represented. If in the parable his example be portrayed in highly emphatic form for didactic purposes and be made to appear exceptional, this is still no argument for the supposed rarity of his prayer in daily life.

The prayer of the tax collector is much different, as his poignant confession of sin and his appeal for mercy so clearly indicate. "Standing far off [he] would not even lift up his eyes to heaven, but beat his breast, saying, 'God, be merciful to me a sinner.'" This is the prayer of a man who is desperate. His behavior reveals his desperation in every way. He stands far off, not finding it within himself to approach the holy place. He is not able even to lift his eyes to heaven, although for normal devotion the uplifted hands would have been the usual posture. Forgetful, if not unaware, of the proper demeanor within the Temple, he beats his breast in the bitter realization of his separation from God. "He and his family are in a hopeless position since for him repentance involves, not only the abandonment of his sinful way of life, i.e., of his calling, but also the restitution of his fraudulent gains plus an added fifth."[8]

In the awful moment of his spiritual crisis, in which his past has become transparent, the tax collector confesses what no man ever wishes to confess—especially from the heart. He confesses that he is a sinner—indeed "the" sinner, in a class by himself.[9] He is bad and he knows it. Yet he also knows that the last resort in such a crisis is a radical honesty before his Maker, unsparingly sincere and concealing nothing. This is why he prays. This is why he has come to the Temple. In such a moment he can expect nothing from the Pharisee, even though they were in the same place praying together. Each is as far from the other as they were under the circumstances of daily life. As for the Pharisee, he is as blind to what is happening in the soul of the tax collector as he is to the condition of his own soul. The strange fact that such a man is standing in the Temple praying so earnestly makes no impression on him. He still goes on thanking God that he is not as the tax collector.

It is important, however, not to misconstrue the nature of the tax collector's confession as if it were a preoccupation with sin comparable to that of the Pharisee with piety. For it is possible to do all that the Pharisee did, but in a negative manner, praying his prayer in reverse and as strongly depreciating oneself as he exalted himself. The degree of egotism would be the same, but its direction would be opposite. Under these circumstances the spiritual significance of such self-depreciation—still an egotistical confession—would be remarkably similar to that of the Pharisee's self-exaltation. This confession would involve the same presumption of laying a claim upon divine favor, except that now it would take the form of a claim upon God's forgiveness. There would still be pride, but pride submerged in the confidence that if the sinner confesses, God will forgive—a pride revealed in its nakedness by the famous skeptic's remark: "Of course God will forgive. That is what he is for."[10]

The significance of the tax collector's prayer would be perverted if in the slightest degree such pride were regarded as secretly motivating him. For what he experienced and the manner in which he threw himself upon the mercy of God do not suggest that he was prompted by such a motive beneath his awareness of sin. His action is too despairingly urgent (existential) to permit such a conclusion. This is why it cannot be regarded as merely an example to copy—as if out of a literalistic desire to fulfill the teaching of Christ the attempt were made to transform it into a rule, a fixed pattern, or even into a litany in which at a given moment all the worshipers in the house of God would be expected to beat their breasts together and to cry out in unison, "God be merciful to me a sinner."

It remains to examine the Pharisee and the tax collector from the perspective of their relative goodness and badness. For it would be wrong to transform the parable into a prosaic lesson on the self-righteousness of the "bad"

Pharisee and the humility of the "good-hearted" tax collector, with the rather inane conclusion that the bad are seldom as bad, and the good seldom as good, as they appear to be. In order to avoid this error, we have to be careful not to condemn the Pharisee too easily, as is popular in proverbial references to hypocrisy of his type. On the basis of conventional standards, ancient or modern, that are popularly maintained as implicit in the accepted way of life, he was a good man. The parable provides little reason for doubting that his appraisal of his achievements was correct. He was a man who had never secured money by coercive, deceitful practices, whose word and deed had always been dependable, and whose personal life had been clean and without unlawful sexual indulgence, which was common enough in ancient Palestine to make his example somewhat exceptional.

In his religious obligations he was undoubtedly exceptional, because whereas others fasted annually, but rarely at other times, he fasted twice a week—on Mondays and Thursdays—which was a rigorous discipline. While others tithed—if at all—only on agricultural products as defined in the sacred law, he tithed not only to this extent but on everything he bought on the market, lest others who by failing to tithe had defiled their produce. In both fasting and tithing he went beyond the requirements of the law, in a form of sacrificial conduct that to him and his countrymen seems to have been a work of supererogation. With such an array of qualifications, his modern counterpart would be welcomed into any respectable community, religious body, or social group and given a responsible position in its life and work. For it is surprising how much egotism and rigorous devotion will be tolerated in a man, if he is just and clean-living and gives of his substance comparable to the tithe of the Pharisee.

But if it is important not to condemn the Pharisee easily, it is equally important not to exalt the tax collector to heights of goodness that his confession in no way suggests. The assumption that we have in him a bad man who all the time had a good heart has no basis in fact. A story-book theme of such a description may have its place in popular journalism, but not in this parable. The awful problem of real sin and sinners has to be accepted for what it is, so that when the tax collector calls himself a sinner because of the rough, sordid background he had no doubt had, we should take him at his word. The fact that he confesses himself as such and throws himself on the mercy of God does not suddenly as if by magic make him good. His change of heart does not change the fact of the wounds and scars that his wretched past has left upon his life and that will always remain. It does not change the fact of wasted time and talent beyond the possibility of being reclaimed. Nor does it change the continual problems of habit and of personal life that cry out for a solution and that will require the slow passage of time if they are ever solved.

Nevertheless, it was this man who in the parable went down to his house justified rather than the other. It was this man who was accepted of God as he was, rather than the Pharisee, who for all his sincerity and sacrifice was not accepted. The crucial distinction between them was not at this point determined by conventional standards of morality but by what had happened or had not happened in the heart of each in relation to God. The goodness of the Pharisee had not changed his heart. Consequently, there was no love at the center of his life toward God or neighbor. His was a strict and serious devotion to holiness that could cherish hatred in the form of a cold, implacable pointing of the finger at the tax collector, who was in the

Temple praying out of the earnestness of a broken spirit. But the badness of the tax collector had not changed his heart either—otherwise more tax collectors would have entered the Temple to pray, because their badness would have precipitated a crisis leading to confession. The truth is that we do not know why the tax collector came to the end of himself and found his way to the Temple. All we know is that a man who throws himself upon the mercy of God in such an unconditional manner, and therefore without presumptions of pleasing him and of winning his favor, is by the grace of God accepted by him. We know this not because of a law, rule, or principle applicable to each situation to determine how God will act but because of the twofold testimony of the Spirit and the Scripture to the faithfulness of God, who does not despise a broken and contrite heart. If in this context we see the meaning of God's faithfulness but dimly, we see it in the cross most clearly, where God gives of himself in the person of his Son for the justification of the ungodly. In the light of the cross, the story of man is ever the same—he that exalteth himself against God even to the highest height of religion will be humbled, while he that humbleth himself before God even to the point of acknowledging no religion will be exalted. The determining factor is the freedom of divine mercy, which in the mysterious working of God is validated in the cross.

Finally, there are certain suggestions concerning the relevance of the parable to the modern religious situation, chiefly in respect to the way in which the separation between the Pharisee and the tax collector bears a resemblance to the separation between the supporters of organized religion and those outside it. The fact, for example, that the Pharisee was identified with a holiness movement dedicated to the preservation of an established form of

religion against the threat of pagan religion and culture—
the ancient equivalent of worldliness—is enough to indicate that his interest in religion was practical. He was
convinced that he was accomplishing a task that was
urgently necessary and as practical as its urgency suggested. In this respect he was representative of that seriousness which may be expressed in a religious concern for
the world but which, as we have already observed, is still
secretly enslaved to egotism and sin under the category of
a goodness whose peculiar prejudice is that it has a monopoly on the presence and favor of God. As a result, it is
really out of touch with the world in spite of its emphasis on practical religion. The conception of a monopoly
operates as a principle of separation to prevent the recognition of any significant action of God elsewhere.

The modern equivalent of the tax collector may be
worshiping in the midst of the church without its recognizing him as the "outsider"[11] who hitherto has had little
interest in religion. His disillusionment with respect to
secularism has enabled him to find in the gospel something that such religion has not yet found. As an outsider,
he has seen too much and too deeply in respect to life and
now in respect to the gospel to be attracted to any form of
religion that merely seeks its own self-justification before
God and, for this very reason, is unable either to understand him or to identify itself with him. In a strange manner he feels rejected in the place where he ought to be
accepted—in the house of prayer, where many persons
though highly religious are yet far from that repentance
which indicates nearness to God. There his past is too
quickly remembered and his poignancy of spirit too
slowly discerned for fellowship with the "insider" to
emerge. There he may hear, if not audibly, then in the
subtle "silent" treatment that speaks more loudly than

words, the prayer of gratitude to God: "I thank thee that I am not as he." In such experiences he will stand alone and misunderstood, unable to find the fellowship of kindred spirits who have discovered in Christ what he has found in him. The gulf which separated the ancient Pharisee and the tax collector in the house of God will separate this "outsider" from the "insider" in the same place and manner.

VI

Surprised by Hell

(Luke 16:19–31)

"There was a rich man, who was clothed in purple and fine linen and who feasted sumptuously every day. And at his gate lay a poor man named Lazarus, full of sores, who desired to be fed with what fell from the rich man's table; moreover the dogs came and licked his sores. The poor man died and was carried by the angels to Abraham's bosom. The rich man also died and was buried; and in Hades, being in torment, he lifted up his eyes, and saw Abraham far off and Lazarus in his bosom. And he called out, 'Father Abraham, have mercy upon me, and send Lazarus to dip the end of his finger in water and cool my tongue; for I am in anguish in this flame.' But Abraham said, 'Son, remember that you in your lifetime received your good things, and Lazarus in like manner evil things; but now he is comforted here, and you are in anguish. And besides all this, between us and you a great chasm has been fixed, in order that those who would pass from here to you may not be able, and none may cross from there to us.' And he said, 'Then I beg you, father, to send him to my father's house, for I have five brothers, so that he may warn them, lest they also come into this place of torment.' But Abraham said, 'They have Moses and the prophets; let them hear them.' And he said, 'No, father Abraham; but if some one goes to them from the dead, they will repent.' He said to him, 'If they do not hear Moses and the prophets, neither will they be convinced if some one should rise from the dead.' "

This is a story of the age-old problem of the rich and the poor, which in any responsible and intelligible approach to the complex of difficulties confronting the modern world must be recognized as basic. The fact that it appears in one of the parables of Jesus suggests that it is essentially a moral and a spiritual problem and not exclusively economic and political. The story begins with sharply contrasted social conditions. There is a rich man clothed in purple and fine linen who feasts luxuriously every day. There is a filthy, festering beggar lying at his gate and living off the garbage from his table. The rich man has everything that money can buy—the best clothing, food, and housing facilities, and the highest status in the community. The beggar is ragged, forgotten, and emaciated—helpless to protect himself against the stray dogs of the street who come licking his sores.

The contrasted social conditions are indicative of contrasting social attitudes. The rich man is indifferent. He lives in luxury, and has no sensitivity to the human misery at his gate. He sees the beggar and yet he does not see him. He knows he is there, but he ignores him. He is immune to shock, to the sight of abject hunger and disease, and to the indignity inflicted upon a fellow being by the dogs of the street. As for the beggar, he is a broken man who has lost all self-regard, and who therefore does not care how he looks or who sees him. He is kept alive by the last vestiges of the organic impulse to live. He has little interest in anything other than the garbage he feeds upon.

The extent to which this story portrays conditions prevalent in first-century Palestine must be recognized if we are to see its relevance in its original setting and in the modern contemporary world. For it was only a little more than a generation after Jesus had included it among his parables that rebellion and warfare swept through the land. This was motivated as much by the insane fury of the oppressed poor against their rich compatriots as by an outraged citizenry against their Roman overlords. The involvement of class strife was but the inevitable logic of history. When the rich, dressed in purple and fine linen, multiply at the expense of beggars like Lazarus, who also multiply, misery must finally revenge itself on those who do not wish to recognize it or do anything about it. The story of what happened in Palestine prior to full-scale war with Rome sounds strangely similar to modern revolutions.

A few glimpses of the situation through the eyes of the Jewish historian Josephus will be sufficiently convincing: "They parted themselves into different bodies, and lay in wait up and down the country, and plundered the houses of the great men, and slew the men themselves, and set the villages on fire; and this till all Judea was filled with the effects of their madness."[12] "The others then set fire to the house of Ananias, the high priest, and to the palaces of Agrippa and Bernice: after which they carried the fire to the place where the archives were deposited, and made haste to burn the contracts belonging to their creditors, and thereby to dissolve their obligations for paying their debts; and this was done in order to gain the multitude of those who had been debtors, and that they might persuade the poorer sort to join in their insurrection with safety against the wealthy; so the keepers of the records fled away, and the rest set fire to them."[13]

It is upon such a background as this—the picture of which is further amplified by those references in the New Testament which speak on the one hand of rich estates with their absentee landlords and on the other of rebellious tenants, dispossessed multitudes, unemployed laborers, and robbers—that we will best understand the parable. The atmosphere is suggested by the accompanying emphasis on the insecurity of possessions and overanxiety for the necessities of life. The story of the rich man and Lazarus is not an incidental story pertaining only to a particular case but a parable of history depicting one of its most persistent and difficult problems.

In the second stage of the story, following the death of both the rich man and the beggar, we are confronted with their different fortunes in the world beyond. Everything is completely reversed and as sharply contrasted as before. Lazarus is carried by the angel servants of God to rest upon Abraham's bosom in heaven, which in Jewish symbolism is the highest place of honor. But the rich man goes to hell, where in indescribable torment he endures the consequences of his indifferent treatment of the beggar during his lifetime. In hell he appeals to Abraham for the slenderest mercy—comparable to a scrap that formerly fell from his table for Lazarus to feed upon—but now asking that merely the tip of the beggar's finger be dipped in water to cool his tongue. In his awful plight, even a drop of water amounts to a fortune, and from the finger of Lazarus it becomes a seeming touch of atonement to assuage his guilt.

But what is this reversal of fortune? Does it ever happen this way? Is there a final rectification that restores the balance of good and evil that come to a man, so that he need only wait and trust that somehow in the end all will be well? Or is it only in dreams and legends and in the religious lore of the nations that the poor triumph and the rich are punished? Is it only ecstasy that declares,

> "He has filled the hungry with good things,
> and the rich he has sent empty away"?
> (Luke 1:53.)

These are the questions a man asks when in the throes of oppression and poverty he sees the everlastingly rich and prosperous wicked. If he is a religious man whose faith is burdened with doubt, his complaint may be that of the psalmist:

"They are not in trouble as other men are;
    they are not stricken like other men. . . .
Their eyes swell out with fatness,
    their hearts overflow with follies.
They scoff and speak with malice. . . .
And they say, 'How can God know?
    Is there knowledge in the Most High?'"
                                            (Ps. 73:5, 7–8a, 11.)

But if he is an irreligious man, he will insist upon these questions and deny the Deity and the beyond and the whole story of the reversal of fortune attributed to the rich man and Lazarus, and denounce it as a deception perpetrated upon the poor.

The issue which at this point will probably confront us is whether the story is vulnerable to the charge that the comfort it affords the poor may be described as an opiate of the people. On this basis, the parable would assure the beggars of the best in the world to come. With this assurance, they may endure their plight in the world of the present. At the same time, it would assure them of the final punishment of the rich, which would sublimate the anger they would otherwise direct at the rich. Interpreted in such a manner, the parable becomes a most effective propaganda weapon of the rich, and more deceptive and captivating of the mind and heart than any other means at their disposal. For even though they are not persuaded of the religion the parable represents, it is to their advantage from this point of view to promote it. For the more beggars persuaded of good things to come in the world beyond, the less trouble they will cause for their masters now.

But this is not the purpose of the parable. It is not designed to comfort beggars. Had it ended with the saying that in his lifetime the rich man had had good things and Lazarus evil things and that the situation was now reversed, this interpretation would have been more plausible. Indeed, Lazarus might have been represented as appealing to Abraham for a messenger to tell his fellow beggars still alive on earth to be content with their misery in view of the heavenly bliss awaiting them. But this is not what happens. The parable moves to a climax in an extended conversation between Abraham and the rich man about the rich man's wealthy brothers who are still alive on earth. Attention is concentrated on his plea that Lazarus be sent to warn these brothers of the awful destiny that awaits them if they do not repent and change their ways. In other words, the parable focuses upon the rich who are still living in luxury and feasting extravagantly, ignoring other beggars at their door. But this is not all. The conversation between Abraham and the rich man turns on a question of particular importance. The point of emphasis is that the rich brothers can be accorded no special privilege by means of a warning that is not available to other people. They are permitted no special messenger from heaven who will single them out and sound a danger signal as if to give them a better chance to repent, presumably because they are rich.

The rich man, of course, would have had it otherwise, as indicated by his persistence in regarding himself as a son of Abraham, with the right of appeal to the spiritual and heavenly head of the covenanted people. Three times he appeals, each time to Father Abraham, as if now, from the heart of hell, he could talk himself out of his judgment or have it modified, or caution others to avoid being caught. But Abraham is not persuaded. He refuses each appeal. For even though the burden of the plea of the man from hell is that of warning his brothers, there is nothing in the parable to suggest that because he was rich he had special influence with God. His brothers are accorded no special favors. Abraham's answer is that they have Moses and the prophets. Let them hear them. The Bible, which they recognize within the scope of their nominal religion but have no interest in obeying (hearing), is a sufficient warning, just as it could have been to the man himself had he chosen to listen to it.

The urgency of the rich man's appeal to Abraham undoubtedly rose from the fact that hell was such a surprise to him—a possibility he had never anticipated. He was at a loss to understand how he could ever have become involved in such an awful predicament. As one who, if not a Sadducee, was possessed of the mentality of a Sadducee, he had apparently assumed that death ends all and that there is no resurrection or judgment. Like those in modern society who have repudiated heaven and hell and the whole question of the beyond in the interests of an exclusive devotion to the present, he apparently had little awareness of destiny and less if any of its determination in every moment. Since any reality that heaven and hell possessed presumably belonged to the present, he could only conclude that his purple and fine linen and his luxurious living were evidence more of heaven than of hell. But the problem which this attitude inevitably created was that he could not recognize the injustice his way of life imposed upon others. In other words, his problem was the same as that of the wealthy everywhere who ignore the beggars at their gates. They are as surprised by, and

as unprepared for, the historical antecedents of hell and
judgment as they presumably will be for the ultimate
form of these, which is integral to the Biblical understanding of destiny. Mesmerized by the spell of immediacy, they evidence an attitude that bears a strange and
sobering resemblance to that of the ancients described
in the Biblical text: "They ate, they drank, they bought,
they sold, they planted, they built, but on the day when
Lot went out from Sodom fire and brimstone rained from
heaven and destroyed them all" (Luke 17:28–29).

As a consequence of the surprise with which the hour
of destiny deals its judgment, the reaction which not infrequently follows is similar to that of the rich man in the
parable. There is a feeling of unfair treatment—a desire to
argue the case at the point of ultimate concern. For the
implication that runs through the rich man's requests of
Abraham is that he himself had not been sufficiently
warned. What he was asking on behalf of his brothers
was by implication what he claimed never to have received himself. And if, moreover, we keep in mind the
significance of Abraham and of the setting in which the
conversation occurred, we will see that the rich man was
really blaming Almighty God for not doing more to save
him. In effect, he was saying that God should have provided a fairer warning. So he wanted to improve upon the
divine procedure by suggesting to Abraham his own solution of the alleged problem of communication.

In this respect, he was not unlike most people of means
who have only a nominal interest in God and religion.
When disaster befalls the system on which their security
depends, they invariably blame religion and not infrequently the hand of Providence for not having done more
to save the situation. With religion considered, from their
point of view, as a means to an end and therefore sub-

ordinate to the established order, and God himself as a patron of that order, to what other conclusion could they come? Or, they will accuse religion of not being bold enough, of not speaking out, and God of not providing some clearer revelation of his purpose and perhaps of not intervening in a spectacular manner at the crucial time. However, although there was probably ample declaration of the word of God under the more secure circumstances preceding the disaster, a strange unwillingness to heed it undoubtedly prevailed. Consequently, we are left with no other alternative than to conclude that the rich will blame religion as readily from their side as the poor from theirs, and for the same reason: it fails to serve their purpose as they conceive it. If the poor accuse religion of possessing a sedative influence (an opiate), the rich will accuse it of failing to act as a stimulant.

It would be wrong to equate riches with sin and poverty with piety, as suggested by the simple, uninterpreted fact that the rich man went to hell and the beggar to heaven. The impression that the former ended in perdition for no other reason than the fact that he was rich, and that the latter ended in glory for no other reason than the fact that he was poor, is a sociological interpretation the Bible does not sanction. For sinfulness and piety would then depend on the socioeconomic class or status with which the individual was identified, in which case the protest against the rich so evident in the Lucan source might be explained away as agrarian or proletarian, and therefore merely relative. The significance of judgment as coming from God and therefore possessed of an absolute quality would then be dissolved, and with it the seriousness that is symbolized by the possibility of heaven and hell.

The protest against the rich which at various times in the history of the Old and New Testaments became so pronounced had as its object the injustice so frequently associated with the procurement of riches, of which the poor in particular were so often the victims. To the prophets and the writers of the wisdom literature whose voices were raised most loudly against the oppressors of the poor it seemed that wealth was so often accumulated by vicious and fraudulent means that it was almost synonymous with sinfulness. The prevalence of ancient Oriental social corruption in the New Testament period, which contributed so largely to the unrest and civil strife that erupted into the Great War with Rome, seemed only to deepen the association between wealth and wickedness, so that Jesus had to say that it was easier for a camel to go through the eye of a needle than for a rich man to enter the Kingdom of God.

The same problem has persisted through the various periods of history to the present day. In spite of notable examples of wealth wisely used, of philanthropic and humanitarian enterprise, and of generous gifts in the public interest, exploitation and the subtle and powerful means by which money dominates the value perspective and possesses the souls of men seem greatly to outweigh the benefits of the generosity of the wealthy. One of the most serious issues of modern times is whether it is possible to amass a fortune by individual or corporate action and do it within the limits of genuine justice. Is it possible to amass a fortune without a Lazarus somewhere either near or far who, as the object of exploitation, becomes the economic base of the accumulated wealth and of the high standard of living associated with it? These are questions which, in the light of the New Testament observation that the love of money is the root of all evils, we can never cease to ponder.

In these various considerations of justice and injustice,

there is one crucial question: What should the rich man have learned—and what had his rich brothers yet to learn —from Moses and the prophets in order to escape the place of torment? Immediately suggesting itself is the answer, running through the whole of the Old Testament Scriptures, that man has an obligation to show mercy toward his neighbor. Such an obligation would include beggars as well as that larger body to whom, according to the Lucan emphasis, Jesus showed particular compassion—the poor, despised, and outcast. That the Old Testament has laid such an obligation upon man will become clear from the insight that all the law and the prophets depend upon two commandments (Matt. 22:40; cf. Gal. 5:14). They may be considered a convenient summary of what is required: You shall love the Lord your God, and your neighbor as yourself.

The reference of the rich man and his brothers to Moses and the prophets could scarcely have meant anything other than this obligation of love in its deepest and richest significance. The obligation would have been laid upon their hearts if they had had any acquaintance with the Scriptures. This conclusion is further supported by the fact that the same two commandments are used in Luke for the introduction of the parable of the good Samaritan, in which the priest and the Levite pass by the wounded man on the road in a manner not unlike that shown by the rich man toward the beggar on his doorstep. Whereas the story of the priest and the Levite pertains only to a single incident, the story of the rich man applies to repeated incidents consolidated into a fixity of attitude and practice. It involves a definite way of life. For it would undoubtedly be the case that he passed Lazarus by as long as he lay at his gate and that he passed him by in his death. Such an evident absence of mercy and of human concern, such calloused indifference, is, according to the Biblical conception of love, as much a sign of godlessness as of inhumanity to man.

The rich man's proposal to Abraham to send Lazarus to give fair warning to his brothers would have been no solution. For to be convinced of the beyond or even of the fact of hell by some indubitable proof such as the return of Lazarus as a ghostlike visitor from the land of the dead would not of itself have transformed the hearts of the rich man's brothers so that their lack of love would have been overcome. The certain knowledge of the beyond would have been no more productive of the repentance necessary to this desirable result than the discovery of an inhabited planet would be productive of love in the hearts of modern men. For the desire to exploit the beyond in its spiritual as well as in its spatial dimension would be just as powerful as the desire to exploit the earth—which, as the strong inclination of men like the rich man's brothers indicates, will continue until conquered by love.

Nor would the awareness of the risk of hell do more than prompt the brothers to substitute another form of exploitation. Anxiety for their ultimate security would only parallel anxiety for their earthly security (riches). Consequently, in any approach to beggars, selfish fear as the predominant motive would prevent the creation of love so necessary for friendship. This is why the truth must be affirmed: "If they do not hear Moses and the prophets, neither will they be convinced if some one should rise from the dead." That love which ultimately means the entrance of Christ into the heart does not possess a man by means of a proof which he demands of God, be it as great a miracle as the resurrection of Christ himself. It comes only by the hearing of the reconciling word of grace out of the Scriptures, as this word points to the beggar on the man's doorstep and in this manner reveals the secret of the resurrection,—of the Christ incarnate as well as of the man and the beggar.

The God of the Bible who asks men to love him and to love one another is himself the God of love, as he is the God of mercy. He is one who identifies himself with the lowly. He is known through the One who with slavelike humility washes the feet of his followers (John 13:2-5), and with the self-same humility is obedient unto death, even death on the cross (Phil. 2:5-8). Under no other sign is it possible to know him except under the sign of lowliness and of suffering love. He is like Lazarus lying on the doorstep of those who would come to know him, or like the man wounded by robbers and left to die on the road of those who would meet him. It is this God whom the rich man could have found in the law and the prophets as they directed him to the beggar on his doorstep—the God extolled in the Magnificat (Luke 1:46-55), who has regarded the low estate of his handmaiden, who has put down the mighty from their thrones and exalted those of low degree, and who has filled the hungry with good things and sent the rich empty away.

VII

The Collapse of Progress
(Luke 12:13–21)

One of the multitude said to him, "Teacher, bid my brother divide the inheritance with me." But he said to him, "Man, who made me a judge or divider over you?" And he said to them, "Take heed, and beware of all covetousness; for a man's life does not consist in the abundance of his possessions." And he told them a parable, saying, "The land of a rich man brought forth plentifully; and he thought to himself, 'What shall I do, for I have nowhere to store my crops?' And he said, 'I will do this: I will pull down my barns, and build larger ones; and there I will store all my grain and my goods. And I will say to my soul, Soul, you have ample goods laid up for many years; take your ease, eat, drink, be merry.' But God said to him, 'Fool! This night your soul is required of you; and the things you have prepared, whose will they be?' So is he who lays up treasure for himself, and is not rich toward God."

Here is a man who believed in progress. He acted only in good and proper fashion, as most men act who own land that brings forth plentifully. He did only what millions do every day as their all-absorbing interest and objective in life. With increased production, he enlarged his storage space. Recognizing the risk of leaving the grain exposed to the weather and to possible theft, he saw to it that ample accommodation was provided. He was evidently a practical man with an eye to business, a wide-

77

awake, aggressive man who undoubtedly arose early in the morning and worked late at night, because a farm of such productivity does not operate by itself. Its plentiful harvests presuppose the industry of its owner. For no matter how fertile the soil and fair the weather, a farm will not cultivate itself or reap the harvest. This always has to be done by the farmer. This farmer was successful because he knew how to plan as well as work. In this respect, his conduct exemplified in such a complete and literal manner what is commonly regarded in modern times as a normal objective in life that it is difficult to expound the parable without a deep awareness of this fact. His desire to pull down his barns and build greater barns is consistent with the progressive spirit of any acquisitive society that pulls down its factories to build greater factories and its old buildings and landmarks to build still greater centers of industry.

Moreover, the farmer's vision of the future was similarly consistent. As his final objective, he looked forward to a time of leisurely retirement in which he could live off his accumulated resources and indulge himself in the sheer pleasure of living. He would really enjoy old age. He would say to himself, "You have ample goods laid up for many years; take your ease, eat, drink, be merry." His objective paralleled that objective which in modern times has become so normal to the so-called abundant life of an affluent society that it is almost universally accepted in one form or another as the goal toward which to strive. Instead of goods laid up for many years, the equivalent value of a pension is presumed to be the guarantee of the pleasurable existence. Accompanying this objective is the same emphasis on leisure and on eating and drinking, with the resulting merriment which in the colloquial spirit of a seemingly carefree existence is described as "having fun." In more sophisticated terms the objective is commonly defined as the pursuit of happiness safeguarded and rendered possible by means of an enduring foundation of material security. In philosophical language, this is the ethic of hedonism. From such a secular point of view, the farmer in the parable can only be praised as a man who was eminently wise and practical because of the provision he made both for himself and for his family. For what he did is what millions are encouraged to do from their youth up by all those agencies in modern society most influential in the determination of popular motives.

But just as he was about to realize his ambition and to retire in comfort, God intervened with the awful indictment, "Fool! This night your soul is required of you." It was more than the fact that he was going to die and that the fruit of his labor would be enjoyed by others—much as the immediacy of the crisis emphasized this painful consequence and reminded him that in actuality he had owned nothing through the years. It was more than the fact of death considered as an event that comes to all men alike and that in unexpected fashion often strikes the busy, successful man before he has reached the final goal of his attainment. It was rather the fact that God was speaking to him out of the experience of his impending death. It was the eternal Word of God breaking through the whole defensive structure of his attitude to life. What mainly suggests such a qualification of the event of his death is the reference to him as "fool." In the Bible, this word is a rare expression, used only with caution because of a peculiar and terrible connotation not associated with the modern use of the word. We can detect this connotation, for example, in the seriousness with which Jesus regards its irresponsible use. In the Sermon on the Mount, he warns, "Whoever says, 'You fool!' shall be liable to the hell of fire." Consequently, when we find the word addressed to the farmer, the seriousness of the divine indictment against him is at once evident. He is under condemnation.

But why? What had he done to deserve such judgment —a man who had always worked hard and efficiently and provided for his family? Why should he have been called a fool, with his reputation for progress and practical-mindedness? Does God reward diligence and the desire to enjoy the fruits of one's labor with angry retribution? Is it a sin to save money and to provide for one's old age? Is there not something so patently unjust in the severity of God's action against this man that the whole modern secular world, in so far as it becomes aware of a similar indictment against itself, will not be inclined to rise up in protest and to disavow such a God?

The answer to these questions is suggested by the Biblical association of "fool" with the kind of life that is indifferent to God—a life which, although not indulging in open and blasphemous denial, amounts to practical atheism. The familiar verse in the psalm will best illustrate the meaning:

> "The fool says in his heart,
> 'There is no God.' "

"In his heart" means in the secret center of his innermost thoughts—the point of origin from which his motives arise. There, a man, his sin unacknowledged and unconfessed, may live, without formal identification with atheistic doctrine or practice, as though the existence of God were fictitious and the only objective in life that of buying and selling, getting and spending. His outlook on life is secular. His practical form of atheism is no different in principle from that of professedly atheistic societies, even though for other reasons he may be violently opposed to them. In this context it is not too much to say that the awful indictment of the farmer in the parable was but an example on a smaller scale of the indictment given in The Book of Daniel. At the height of the grandiose feast of Belshazzar the strange handwriting appeared on the wall: "God has numbered the days of your kingdom and brought it to an end; . . . you have been weighed in the balances and found wanting; . . . your kingdom is divided and given to the Medes and Persians" (Dan. 5:26–28).

The occasion of the parable will throw further light on its interpretation. A man had approached Jesus with the request that he persuade his brother to divide his inheritance with him. Apparently a disagreement had arisen in the settlement of the family estate. If an older brother had received the landed property, according to the traditional practice, the man who questioned Jesus might have been a younger brother dissatisfied with the share of salable goods accorded him. Under these circumstances, he would come to Jesus as to any rabbi in the hope of securing a favorable decision. It is possible that he had seen in Jesus' attitude to the law and tradition what he had mistakenly regarded as a form of leverage he could use against his brother to force a decision. At any rate, Jesus saw his problem not as a bona fide case of injustice but as a case of covetousness that deserved the rebuke, "Man, who made me a judge or divider over you?"—to which he added for a larger company, "Take heed, and beware of all covetousness: for a man's life does not consist in the abundance of his possessions." At this point Jesus tells the parable—evidently as a warning against such covetousness.

In order to appreciate the warning, it is necessary to consider the probable connection between covetousness and the practical atheism to which it leads. Expressed in a few words, covetousness is a form of lust characterized by the total manner in which it prompts a man to devote his life to possessions. The inventive and productive skill of modern man and the resulting easy availability of possessions have only intensified man's anxious, acquisitive appropriation of things. A multitude of things constitutes the ultimate goal representing as it were a conglomerate god—so that the conviction steadily grows that a man's life does consist in the abundance of things possessed and that these are a measure of his worth.

Because others are seen less as persons than as things, the whole complexity of human relationships is incorporated into the conglomerate god in the form of numbers, commodities, and customers. Friendships are perverted into sources of influence and persons are seen only in the light of their money value. As life is thus depersonalized, real love gradually disappears because the ability to love atrophies and is eventually lost. With this loss, the all-important insight into the depths of human life, which is the substance of wisdom, also disappears. Man is emptied of himself in a process that can produce only a hollow man—a thing without a soul, eventually without a heart, and finally without a mind. But he never wholly succeeds in reaching this stage, reacting with an ironical longing to eat, drink, and be merry. It is within this strange and profound alienation from love that practical atheism emerges. Such atheism is consistent with the Biblical observation, "He who does not love does not know God; for God is love" (I John 4:8).

If this process did not affect the farmer in the parable to the same extent or in the precise form in which it does his counterpart in the present day, it should in no way detract from the seriousness of the practical atheism that defined his attitude toward destiny. For if he conceived of the ultimate goal of life to be of eating, drinking, and making merry, it is obvious that we should add the remainder of this ancient adage: "for tomorrow we die." In this additional phrase lie both the real meaning of what is involved in being transformed into a thing and the real source of irony in the longing for pleasure. The farmer, it would seem, had accepted the inevitable fact of death, but by that acceptance he had provided himself with a certain defense against death. He expected to die, according to plan—in his own good time, as it were. After a period of pleasure, in which he could fully satisfy himself on the fruits of his labor, and after the final feast of life, when he would be drowsy from satiation, it would seem most natural to die, as if merely falling asleep after a heavy meal.

In accordance with such a conception, death was one item of life among many—something included within his understanding of life and for which he was ready, provided always that it came at the end of life as he had defined it and that he first be permitted to extract the most from life so as to justify his existence to himself before the final injustice against him. The longing for pleasure was, on this basis, a compensatory function that betrayed the extent to which his life was unlived at every stage. It was like a gradually accumulating debt over the years, which he hoped to pay off at last in the currency of sensual satisfaction. But strictly speaking, the debt could not be paid off, because of the impossibility of recovering the unlived portion of any stage of life. He had irrevocably lost those unlived portions of life because of the necessity of building barns. In this respect, a crisis was already implicit in his life before he heard the call of God, which exposed his life and precipitated his death in the decisive manner described.

The concluding comment of the parable (Luke 12:21) poses the question implicit in it from the beginning: What does it mean to be rich toward God? He whose chief purpose in life was to pull down barns and build larger barns has by his example unwittingly emphasized the question that inevitably emerges when men identify themselves with things: Of what does real wealth consist? This question, when pondered, soon reminds us that we have entered the realm of the intangible where, because there is nothing to be laid hold upon and counted and measured, there is little promise of genuine wealth or benefit. It is a realm in which all things have a way of becoming permissible unless a careful eye is kept on them. There are grounds for suspicion that the intangible is real only in the doubtful dreams of men and has no correspondence in ultimate fact. For the pulling down of dreams to build greater dreams is characterized by a subtler foolishness than that of the farmer, who could at least distinguish barns from dreams. Yet, for all our precaution, there is one thing of which we are certain—in the Bible from beginning to end it is unequivocally asserted that he who is rich toward God is incomparably rich. He possesses the greatest of treasures—a treasure incorruptible and secure from every form of seizure and beside which all secular wealth fades into insignificance. What does this mean?

Expressed in simple terms, a man who is rich toward God, rather than possessing his treasure in the form of money, goods, and property, is himself the treasure. Like a child awakened to love by the love of his parents, who recognize him as precious, the man who is rich toward

God is awakened to love by the love of God, who sees him as precious. It is as the Scripture affirms: "We love, because he first loved us." This is the form of love that includes the brother, inasmuch as "he who loves God should love his brother also." In other words, the man who is rich toward God becomes truly a man, a human being whose integrity and genuineness are authenticated by both his friends and his foes. And should the validity of such intangible wealth be doubted, we need only consider what happens to the country whose people fail to manifest it in themselves and possess their wealth only in the form of money, goods, and property. Each person distrusts the other and conceals his motives under a façade of unreality, until at length he hardly knows himself. In its extreme form, such distrust causes each person to begin in various ways to devour the other with a bestial lack of sensitivity, and human life is cheapened and degraded. The familiar lines of the poet describe the process: "Ill fares the land to hastening ills a prey where wealth accumulates and men decay."[14]

It cannot be claimed, however, that any deity will so work in a man that he himself constitutes his treasure— will so enter into him that his life will manifest the integrity tantamount to genuine but intangible wealth. Since "there are many 'gods' and many 'lords'" but one Lord, Jesus Christ (I Cor. 8:5–6), we cannot say that any god will do. Instead, we have to be careful about the identity of the God whose power with respect to man will produce such a result. For some persons conceive of a deity whose principal function is the safeguarding of the ultimate interests of a man like the farmer in the parable. Instead of declaring a man's doom, such a deity would come to his aid and give him the heartiest welcome beyond the vale of tears, as if to extend forever, in the form of a heavenly feast, his eating and drinking and making merry. Such a deity would say of him, precisely because of his propensity for barns, "Well done, good and faithful servant; . . . enter into the joy of your master" (Matt. 25:23). By the same token, this deity would welcome the poor to the same feast not as an extension of earthly riches and pleasure but as a compensation for the lack of them. In this ultimate form, the conception of what is good for the poor would be no different in principle from the conception of what is good for the rich. Covetousness, which afflicts both those who have and those who do not have, would be unchallenged in the lives of each group. But such a deity would not be the God of the Bible who by His power is able so to work in a man that he himself constitutes his treasure independently of what he may otherwise possess. Such a deity would be only an idol, a patron of covetousness.

In all these considerations, it must be remembered that a treasure is no treasure if it does not endure. The farmer in the parable could not take his wealth with him. It slipped out of his hands. It was left behind. But this was not the only way it might have vanished. It might have been wasted by mismanagement, expropriated, devaluated, depleted by taxation, destroyed, or stolen—to mention the commoner ways in which wealth vanishes. In this respect, the wealth of the farmer was wealth only for a time. It had the ephemeral quality of the mist, which disappears with the heat of the day, or of the color of the rainbow, which fades. But if the treasure into which a man is transformed by the love of God is equally ephemeral, so that it too vanishes in death, it is no real treasure, but it is as illusory as the barns the farmer had to leave behind. By the same token, the love of God would be as ephemeral as all other love under the same circumstances, so that in the death of the man would be the death of love. This would mean that love is in the same category as the eating and drinking and making merry, which ceased with him. It is therefore axiomatic in the Biblical understanding of a man's being constituted a treasure that such an event is the gift of God to and for the man. It is a gift that transforms him—a gift more frequently described as eternal life, which is not ephemeral, nor illusory, nor merely a function of the bodily or psychical constitution of the man himself. Instead, it is a new life, untouched by death and equally untouched by the sin that leads to death—a new life that is but the divine assertion of the claim that the man belongs to the God who made him. This new life is the sign of the resurrection in its rich and radical and mysterious reality. This was what the farmer in the parable did not have. This is why he was a fool.

VIII

Necessary Worldliness

(Luke 16:1–8)

"There was a rich man who had a steward, and charges
were brought to him that this man was wasting his goods.
And he called him and said to him, 'What is this that I hear
about you? Turn in the account of your stewardship, for you
can no longer be steward.' And the steward said to himself,
'What shall I do, since the master is taking the stewardship
away from me? I am not strong enough to dig, and I am
ashamed to beg. I have decided what to do, so that people
may receive me into their houses when I am put out of the
stewardship.' So, summoning his master's debtors one by one,
he said to the first, 'How much do you owe my master?' He
said, 'A hundred measures of oil.' And he said to him, 'Take
your bill, and sit down quickly and write fifty.' Then he said
to another, 'And how much do you owe?' He said, 'A hundred
measures of wheat.' He said to him, 'Take your bill, and write
eighty.' The master commended the dishonest steward for his
prudence; for the sons of this world are wiser in their own
generation than the sons of light."

Men often do desperate things in a crisis. Not infrequently they disregard the restraints of law and conscience and indulge in conduct which under normal circumstances would be foreign to them. If it is a situation
involving self-defense, they will not hesitate to kill. If it is
a question of vital necessities, they will not hesitate to

steal. If it is a matter of preserving appearances for the
sake of pride, they will often pretend and sacrifice until
they reach a point where they would rather die than have
their artificial world collapse upon them.

In the case of the steward in the parable, he had just
been informed of his dismissal and of the necessity of
rendering an account of his practices. This, as we know
from the social conditions of ancient Palestine during the
first century of the Christian era, was no less of a crisis
than in modern times when the specter of unemployment
may confront a man with an emergency of serious magni-
tude. Nor was the distress of the steward mitigated by the
knowledge that his dismissal was the consequence of his
own mismanagement and that such action on the part of
his employer was wholly justified. The situation was only
made worse because, in addition to the distress of unemployment, he had himself to blame. Other possible em-
ployers interested in securing his services would hear of
his failure, and soon none of them would want him. If,
moreover, under the circumstances of Jewish society the
steward was a trusted slave in charge of an estate or of a
sizable business, his dismissal would be even worse. For
in view of the generally favorable treatment accorded
under Jewish law to slaves, who in many instances were
regarded as part of the family and had coveted privileges,
his dismissal would be as disastrous as a son's being dis-
inherited by his father. It would be a calamity. He would
be set free only to wander from place to place and perhaps
to starve under the stigma of disgrace.

The question that confronted the steward demanded
quick and courageous action. What was he to do? The
time was short, his security jeopardized, and his future in
doubt. Associated as he was with the upper class, and
never having engaged in work involving heavy muscular

exertion, manual labor from his point of view was out of the question. Moreover, in his particular specialty the opportunities of employment were extremely limited. All this and more was evident in the peculiar pride that moved him to exclaim, "I am not strong enough to dig, and I am ashamed to beg." Accordingly, he felt that the only alternative was to make the most of the situation and to act before his employer had time to effect his dismissal.

Consequently, while he still had authority as general manager, he proceeded as quickly as possible to write off a substantial proportion of the debt each customer owed. This, of course, had nothing to do with the common procedure in bankruptcy of allowing the creditor a certain percentage of the amount he would have otherwise received. It was the other way around—the manager gave away the owner's money without permission by easing the obligations of his debtors, and this for no other reason than to win their favor so that eventually they would return the favor by employing him. It was a plain case of fraud, which by any standard was a high-handed act. Because it followed a record of waste and inefficiency, and happened so soon after his dismissal, it was insult added to injury. And it is hardly necessary to say that the debtors were willing enough to oblige. They were not repelled by the unscrupulous nature of his action. The particulars are clear from the text: "So, summoning his master's debtors one by one, he said to the first, 'How much do you owe my master?' He said, 'A hundred measures of oil.' And he said to him, 'Take your bill, and sit down quickly and write fifty.' Then he said to another, 'And how much do you owe?' He said, 'A hundred measures of wheat.' He said to him, 'Take your bill, and write eighty.'"

At this point the story stops abruptly with the comment that the master commended the dishonest steward for his prudence. This prudence, of course, was worldly prudence, or shrewdness. It involved astute financial maneuvering, in which the advantage went to the man of wits who acted quickly. But who was the master who commended him? This has always been the snag on which the interpreter has stumbled and which trips up the smooth flow of exposition. Moreover, the series of moralistic statements that follow suggests the embarrassment experienced within the Christian community from the beginning about the real point of the parable. If the master was the employer, a word of commendation from the lips of one so obviously victimized would be strange, particularly when it is unaccompanied by the kind of qualifying phrase that a man in such a mood would be inclined to add. And even if, on his part, there was a certain fascination for such rascality, it is unlikely he would be so forthright in his praise.

The other possibility is that the master was Jesus himself—an interpretation sufficiently offensive from the beginning that for this reason it should be regarded as the more probable one. This, of course, cannot be pressed. But whatever the answer, it is not too difficult to understand how Jesus interpreted the action of the steward. For here was a man in a critical situation who did something about it. Dishonest as his action was, he saw what was coming and acted quickly and to the best advantage for himself, using the only wisdom he possessed. He was a realist who did not fold his arms and lament his lot and begin blaming his employer and the state of the world for what had happened. Jesus would be quick to see the spiritual counterpart of such action—what it would be like if transformed into the decisiveness of a faith as realistic with respect to the larger predicament of man as this rascal had been with respect to his predicament.

By thus interpreting the parable as an appeal for decisive faith, it could well be that Jesus originally addressed it to the unconverted—the indifferent, doubtful, and hesitant of spirit comprising so many in the common crowd.[15] To these persons, the bold rascality of the steward would possess that same quality of newsworthiness which in modern times would probably obtain a headline. This is not an unreasonable inference, judging from two other incidents recorded in Luke. They were of an equally sensational character and were the subject of popular interest. One incident was Pilate's massacre of the Galileans, when he mingled their blood with their sacrifices, and the other was the collapse of the Tower of Siloam, with the loss of eighteen workmen. In both instances, popular opinion speculated on whether the victims were worse-than-average sinners because of the nature of their death, but apparently avoided any suggestion of a similar judgment on itself. Then, as now, massacres, accidents, and fraudulent actions were of popular interest—but seldom the means of causing the idle mind to stop and think and seriously interpret his own situation. Instead of letting the total impression of such events sober him into a realization of their spiritual significance—events that in modern times comprise so large a part of the daily news—he lets them pass with a strange indifference. They are all events out there which affect other persons only. They do not touch him.

If, as is likely, this was the popular reaction to the dishonesty of the steward, Jesus seems to have disposed of the reaction in the same manner in which he disposed of the speculation about the victims of Pilate's massacre

and of the falling Tower of Siloam. Instead of focusing
upon the guilt of the steward and condemning his conduct, as the critical spectator would do, he focused specifically upon the spiritual relevance of the steward's conduct for the spectator himself and generally upon the potential value of that conduct as a means of communicating
the evangel. The precise manner in which his interpretation accomplished this objective is far from clear. However, it is easy to imagine the effect of his appearance, in a
similar manner, before a modern audience. With the news
of the day in hand, he would caution against a judgmental attitude that decries the wickedness of the world
but fails to see the same wickedness in itself—and fails
even more to appreciate the prudence of those it con-
demns. For although the world is what it is, with its daily
record of scandal, there is often an amazing manifestation
of shrewd maneuvering, of studied devices for gaining
advantage in questionable areas of business and politics,
and, quite often, of quick discernment of a threat to
material security.

But the tragedy is that the same sagacity is not exhibited toward the real predicament, which the illusion
of pleasant surroundings, health and strength, material
security and social status, does so much to conceal. For
there is the unrighteousness each man shares with the
world in which he lives, and for which he is responsible
no matter how indifferent he may be to faith in God.
Though he may be totally absorbed in buying and selling,
in getting and spending, he shall not escape. Though his
perspective may be foreshortened and his interests confined to the immediacy of the present, and though he may
have no thought of the vast world in which he lives or of
the problem of destiny, he shall not be absolved. Though
he may hide behind his questions, defend himself by argu-

ment, shield himself with a plausible way of life, and resort to all manner of subterfuge, and though he may even shrug his shoulders with the excuse that there is nothing he can do, he shall not be spared. As a human being, he is in a predicament. A question mark for which in a strange manner he himself is responsible is written in bold letters over the whole of his existence. That question mark is more than a matter of war and hydrogen bombs and the future of the nation and of civilization. It is a deep and muffled interrogation which stirs from within the heart and which at times moves him to murmur in a language peculiar to himself and even to cry out on some variation of the theme: Why? What does it all mean? Who am I? What is to become of me and of my fellow men?

At this point the important consideration is whether the man aware of the interrogation will respond with at least the shrewdness he exhibits in other and less serious situations. The practical prudence that serves him so well in everyday life, and that prompts him to explore every conceivable solution when he finds himself in a corner from which there is no exit, ought to serve him in this predicament. Even though he has never troubled himself with the church, or cared for religion, or prayed, or read his Bible, or considered his Maker, if he exhibits half the concern he does in escaping the situations that affect his immediate welfare, he will know what to do in this situation. Even a thief, who like the unjust steward in the parable is not inhibited by moral considerations, will have sense enough to know what he ought to do.

In this respect, the practical prudence that ought to persuade man to turn to God, if he is half as shrewd as he is in business, industry, politics, and social life, has been compared in the Old Testament to the simple understand-

ing of an animal in its knowledge of the hand that feeds
it. Isaiah says:

> "The ox knows its owner,
>> and the ass its master's crib;
> but Israel does not know,
>> my people does not understand."
>>> (Isa. 1:3.)

Or to take an example from The Proverbs, even an ant in
the ant hill can teach the spiritual sluggard how he ought
to respond to his predicament in the presence of God.

> "Go to the ant, O sluggard;
>> consider her ways, and be wise.
> Without having any chief,
>> officer or ruler,
> she prepares her food in summer,
>> and gathers her sustenance in harvest."
>>> (Prov. 6:6–8.)

If the ox and the ass and the ant at their simple level of
wisdom respond as they do, how much more should man
respond to the question affecting his destiny.

The faith of the man who turns to God out of desperation because, like the steward in the parable, he finds no
other way out does not possess, of course, the high, rich
quality of insight that is characteristic of spiritual ma-
turity, but this faith should not be despised. For although it provides only the slenderest thread of hope to
the man who clutches it, it is the difference between life
and death. And although it is often laid hold upon blindly
out of confusion and despair as from the proverbial leap
in the dark, it is the confidence that, however deeply the
soul may sink, the merciful arm of God will rescue it at

the bottom. Selfish though such prudence may appear to be, it is still a man's commitment of himself to God, which, like the thief on the cross, is accepted with the amazing promise: "Today you will be with me in Paradise." Accordingly, it is always well to remember that such faith has more in common with mature faith than appearances suggest, because even mature faith is always like the faith of Abraham of old, who "went out, not knowing whither he went."

Least of all should those who readily identify themselves with the realm of the moral and spiritual despise such prudence, for it was Israel whom the prophet compared with the ox and the ass—to the advantage of the ox and the ass. And it was those possessed of light and too quick to judge whom Jesus compared with the unjust steward—to his advantage.

IX

No Facile God

(Luke 11:5–8; 18:1–8)

And he said to them, "Which of you who has a friend will
go to him at midnight and say to him, 'Friend, lend me three
loaves; for a friend of mine has arrived on a journey, and I
have nothing to set before him'; and he will answer from
within, 'Do not bother me; the door is now shut, and my children are with me in bed; I cannot get up and give you anything'? I tell you, though he will not get up and give him
anything because he is his friend, yet because of his impor-
tunity he will rise and give him whatever he needs."

And he told them a parable, to the effect that they ought
always to pray and not lose heart. He said, "In a certain city
there was a judge who neither feared God nor regarded man;
and there was a widow in that city who kept coming to him
and saying, 'Vindicate me against my adversary.' For a while
he refused; but afterward he said to himself, 'Though I neither
fear God nor regard man, yet because this widow bothers me,
I will vindicate her, or she will wear me out by her continual
coming.'" And the Lord said, "Hear what the unrighteous
judge says. And will not God vindicate his elect, who cry to
him day and night? Will he delay long over them? I tell you,
he will vindicate them speedily. Nevertheless, when the Son of
Man comes, will he find faith on earth?"

The widow in the second parable was evidently the victim of injustice—probably at the hands of a rich and

influential man. The circumstances of her case suggest that it was a money matter—perhaps a debt, a pledge, or a portion of an estate was being withheld from her. To make it worse, the judge was a hardened character who cared nothing for God or man. All he cared about was procuring a handsome bribe. Since she was too poor to give a bribe, her only weapon was persistence. If she could make a sufficient nuisance of herself, she might wear him down to the point where he would give her what she wanted. According to the parable, her strategy was successful. The judge relented. Though he admitted that he had no concern for God or man, and therefore no concern for justice, yet as the widow continued pestering him he yielded to her plea and gave her justice simply to get rid of her.

A similar theme runs through the parable of the unwilling neighbor. An unexpected guest arrives at the home of a friend late at night. The friend, who is presumably poor and living from hand to mouth with only enough to feed his family a day at a time, is caught. He has nothing in the cupboard. And since, according to Eastern custom, he is obliged to entertain a guest, he has no alternative but to knock on the door of his neighbor at midnight and ask for a loan of loaves. He has to do it no matter how embarrassing it is. The neighbor, however, is unwilling. He does not want to be bothered. It is late at night. He and his family are all asleep on the mat in their one-room peasant's house. To rise and unbolt the door will make a lot of noise and wake everyone up. However, he finally yields—not because he wants to do it, but only for the sake of appearance. He cannot have it said that a friend came to his door late at night for bread and was turned away.

These parables have to do not with a trite moral lesson

on piety but with faith in God when, to all intents and purposes, he seems to be unresponsive to the cry of his people. The fact that the judge is depicted as unjust and the neighbor as unwilling, far from being incidental to to the interpretation, coincides with the nature of this problem. For the man of faith whose soul is cast down for want of a recognizable response to the desperate cry of his need does wonder if God is not unjust, if it is not difficult to arouse him from behind a door that is closed and barred. At times the man of faith may be tempted to ask, "What is the good of believing in God?" or with the ancient psalmist: "How long, O Lord? Wilt thou forget me forever?" (Ps. 13:1). Rather than try to eliminate the offense of these parables by avoiding the slightest suggestion that God could bear any resemblance to the unjust judge or the unwilling neighbor, it seems preferable to recognize this possibility.

Jesus not infrequently used such a procedure to arrest the attention of his hearers and to bring home to them some aspect of his teaching that required decisive thought. We need only recall the use he made of such noteworthy examples as the scandalous action of the dishonest steward, the questionable generosity of the father to the prodigal, the inequity of the farmer who paid his men the same wage at the end of the day for differing amounts of labor, and the resemblance of the coming of the Son of Man to the coming of a burglar in the night. When each example is measured by the strict rules of justice and of appropriate comparison, a certain unfairness is evident that leaves the hearer puzzled—the more so because the example pertains to God. On this basis, the parables of the unjust judge and of the unwilling neighbor illustrate the way in which God may appear to his people when, having turned to him in their adversity, they are prompted to wonder at his slowness to intervene. Their problem is the same as that of the ancient martyrs who out of great tribulation cried unto him, "How long before thou wilt judge and avenge our blood on those who dwell upon the earth?" Such a cry can still be heard from the concentration camps of modern nations.

Naturally, the interpreter hesitates to represent God in such a manner, because such representation is suggestive of irreverence. To reflect seriously on the unjust judge and the unwilling neighbor as symbolical of the divine seems to border on blasphemy. How dare we think of God as unjust or unwilling to help, when according to the popular image he is never severe or critical? How dare we think otherwise when we have so often been assured that he is always nice and kind?

But for all that may be said of the emphasis that ought to be put on the love of God, it is never so easy as this. God is not a mere projection of domestic virtue. He is never known in the facile manner in which one man may know another. He is known only in mystery. (Rom. 11:33–36.) If we have any doubt of this, the cry of dereliction from the cross, expressed in the language of the ancient psalmist, ought to set us thinking. "My God, my God, why hast thou forsaken me?" The fact that Jesus uttered these words while hanging on the cross, condemned to be slain after the manner of a common criminal, and that this crucifixion could be represented as involving a mysterious act of God, will seem even more irreverent. What kind of god but one who is unjust according to the strict rules of human justice could be privy to such a sacrifice? If we cavil at the unjust judge and the unwilling neighbor because they represent a certain appearance of divinity, the cross represents even more profoundly the same problem, because its offense consists in its shattering of facile conceptions of deity.

The problem, however, is broader than the problem of the persecuted man of faith who pleads with God to intervene. His experience is representative of a more pervasive feeling on the part of the faithful, irrespective of the possibility of persecution or martyrdom. For when they cry, "How long, O Lord?" it is often because of a general impression that much of life is against them. Their existence is posited in struggle. Without the will to live, they die. But even with the will to live, when they consider nature's indifference to the rules of human justice they wonder if the whole of life is not unjust. As they work and love and sacrifice, the same indifference makes them wonder whether these achievements will count, or their lives will count, or anything will count in the end. Or will everything be swallowed up in oblivion —an oblivion that makes mockery of all their effort and seriousness and constitutes in this respect the worst injustice? As the widow persisted for the payment of a debt in the hope of justice from an unjust judge, so they persist for a life and a world in the hope of justification before what seems at least like an unkind fate. If all is ultimately empty, who can live? Who can live who in living finds no end for which to live—no end that is not a life that counts? Only to count—that is the hope for which they strive—to find some justification not for this or that but for the whole of existence. For they believe that somehow there is justice, somewhere a justification that will prove that nature's indifference is not final. Like the widow before the judge and the friend at the door of the unwilling neighbor, they refuse to give up. Faith prompts them to say:

"Why are you cast down, O my soul,
        and why are you disquieted within me?
Hope in God; for I shall again praise him."
                                        (Ps. 42:11.)

But even if God were like the unjust judge or the unwilling neighbor, there would still be hope. For the fact
cannot be denied that the unexpected happened—the unjust judge pronounced judgment in favor of the widow,
and the unwilling neighbor gave bread to the man at his
door. Their motives were far from the best—the one
feared that the pestering of the widow would weary him,
the other feared that he would lose face—but their action
procured the benefits most desired by those who waited
upon them. In each case, what happened was contrary to
appearances. Both the judge and the neighbor acted on
the whim of the moment. An hour later each might have
been in a different mood. As this possibility suggests, their
action was considerably a matter of chance, and almost
anyone would benefit who had the courage to persist. To
put it in modern phraseology, eventually his ticket would
be drawn. In some cases the chances would be better, in
other cases it would be poorer, but whatever the circumstances might be there would always be a possibility of
winning. For the mystery of contingency is as legitimate
an aspect of life as the laws of necessity. Indeed, on this
basis it can be said that "you . . . , who are evil, know how
to give good gifts to your children" (Luke 11:13). The
good gifts are a kind of fortuitous exception—a senti-
mental, mood of the moment, thing-to-do, giving that is
an exception to the basically selfish pattern of life. In the
modern setting, such giving is often whimsical to the point
of rewarding such persons as actors and entertainers out
of all proportion to those whose services are of the most

enduring benefit to posterity. Or it will reward its children as much to keep them silent as for any other reason. And yet for all this, fortuitous though it may be, we cannot deny the benefits it provides.

A god who gave gifts in this manner, even though a whimsical god of this world, in his moments of goodness could still be the source of many benefits. Speaking of nature as a deity, the same could be said. Though "red in tooth and claw" with blood, though indifferent to human values, this goddess would still have her seasons of fortuitous goodness—a goodness which the farmer knows from his gamble with the elements. But good health and harvests would eventuate, even though finally the goddess saw to it that death had the last word and that the voice of the petitioner was effectively silenced. On this basis, the god or goddess of this world would be served by a faith that was daring enough to look for the colloquial "breaks" and to contrive by all its science and art to improve the prospect of taking advantage of them. It would harbor the optimistic assumption that there is always a way out. It would encourage the assumption that if a man is lucky, his god is with him; if unlucky his god is against him. In either case, divine favor is measured merely by whether or not his skin is saved. Nevertheless, out of such a conception of life a certain justice would emerge, as well as a certain measure of relief like that obtained by the widow and the man at the door.

But the cry of the elect is not the cry of those who depend upon such a god. It is not the cry of those who hope to take advantage of some unexpected change in his mood. It is not the cry of those who believe in the deification of chance. This is why we must not place the emphasis upon the persistence of the widow or of the friend as though everything depended on human initiative's exploiting the mystery of contingency. Instead, the crying of the elect is like the cry of children to a father, who in their innocence turn to him with no ulterior motives in mind. It is like the crying of the beggar Lazarus in the extremity of his need, or the fervent appeal of the tax collector praying in the Temple, or the moaning of the beaten, half-dead man at the side of the road—always utterly realistic, bereft of security, disillusioned and knowing that there is nothing other to depend upon but God, and for this reason discovering what faith should always mean and what it is to pray.

Consequently, the elect do not know why they persist. Their persistence is not grounded in itself. They pray, but not in their own strength. It is not the natural quality of persistence sustained as it were by will power, as if the main lesson of the parables is that each man must secure what he wishes by pushing for it and in the end answering his own prayers. For how far does a man get by answering his own prayers in the face of nature's indifference or of the enigma of death, both of which pose for him the problem of ultimate justification? Instead, the cry of the elect is better explained by the pull from beyond (grace) than by the push from within, because it persists with a strange foolishness despite everything to the contrary. Its confidence is like the prophetic hope so beautifully expressed in the words of Habbakuk:

> "Though the fig tree do not blossom,
>   nor fruit be on the vines,
> the produce of the olive fail
>   and the fields yield no food,
> the flock be cut off from the fold
>   and there be no herd in the stalls,

yet I will rejoice in the Lord,
I will joy in the God of my salvation."
(Hab. 3:17–18.)

The cry of the elect is therefore the cry of the Israel of God—that enigmatic people of every age, so hard to understand, so contradictory of behavior, so often despised and rejected of men and acquainted with grief. It is the cry of that Israel so well represented by the poor, the widow, and the fatherless, the underdog, and the outcast, whether we are thinking of the Old Israel of the Old Testament or the New Israel of the New Testament, or of the lost sheep of the house of Israel, ancient or modern. It is the cry of the people of the land, still daring to pray though ostracized by scribes and Pharisees, or the cry of the unchurched from the no man's land of faith and unbelief in the modern world. The Israel of God of every description—that thin red line of the faithful through every age whose peculiar role is to be the suffering servants of the One who is the author and finisher of such a role—cry at the gate of justice for this very reason. As the object of Jesus' special concern in the parables of Luke, and, as such, the representatives of the people of God in the ancient past and the modern present, they are those who are broken and contrite in spirit. They are those who bear the offense of their God according to the apostolic description: "For consider your call, brethren; not many of you were wise according to worldly standards, not many were powerful, not many were of noble birth; but God chose what is foolish in the world to shame the wise, God chose what is weak in the world to shame the strong, God chose what is low and despised in the world, even things that are not, to bring to nothing things that are, so that no human being might boast in the presence of God" (I Cor. 1:26–29). These are they who cry day and night unto him.

The assurance Jesus gives is that the God to whom they appeal is by nature one who will vindicate them. God does not need to be prompted to do so. Vindication is his purpose for them—and through them for the world in which they live. It is in no sense exceptional. The way in which Jesus framed his question indicates that any other possibility would be unthinkable. His question expects an affirmative answer: "And will not God vindicate his elect, who cry to him day and night?" The added assertion emphasizes it: "I tell you, he will vindicate them speedily." Although God may appear like the unjust judge or the unwilling neighbor, he is quite different from any form of deity they might conceivably represent. Even at best, considering the most that men might derive on the basis of probability from such deities, indeed from the natural world the goodness of God is much more than this. The comparative form of the question—"How much more . . .?" (Luke 11:13)—as it pertains to the Heavenly Father, is indicative of this fact. If those who are evil can give good gifts to their children, how much more can the people of God expect of Him who is altogether righteous? The difference here is more than one of degree, as if God gives only to a greater extent. It is decidedly one of a kind, so that ultimately there is no comparison.

As one who has bound himself to his people and they to him so that he can speak of them as his own, he is the hearer and answerer of their prayers. In his freedom he wills to hear and respond to their petitions and encourages them to turn to him. There is no ambiguity in the Bible about this matter. "He hears the prayer of the righteous." (Prov. 15:29.) "The Lord is near to all who call upon

him, to all who call upon him in truth." (Ps. 145:18.) Or
if we wish assurance from the sayings associated with the
parables under discussion, what is better than Jesus' exhortation: "Ask, and it will be given you; seek, and you
will find; knock, and it will be opened to you" (Luke
11:9)? If, with these assurances of the readiness of God
for his people, we take the saying of Jesus that God will
vindicate them speedily, the actual situation is different
from what it seems. Instead of being unresponsive to his
people, God is quick to respond. Instead of being slow to
hear, he is sensitive to their cry. So far from being hard to
arouse from behind a door that is closed and barred, he
stands at the open door.

But why is Jesus so forthright in his assurance that God
is ready to hear the cry of his people and to respond on
their behalf? Why does he say that God will vindicate
them speedily when they cry unto him day and night for
help? There is such a sharp contrast with what seems to
be the case from their point of view. The answer lies in the
fact that Jesus took so seriously the action of God in his
own life and ministry. He was deeply conscious of God's
acting in and through his actions. He was equally aware
of the action of God in the history of Israel and in the
world around him. This is why he could speak so de-
cisively about the ease with which people could interpret
the sky for signs of fair or foul weather but fail to discern
the signs of the times (Luke 12:54–56; cf. Matt. 16:1–3).

The signs of the times had to do with evidence of the
action of God, which, according to the tradition of the
Bible from beginning to end, is evident in history and in a
particular way in the history of God's own people. This is
what his elect had to see in order to be encouraged—a
new awareness of the presence of God, i.e., the Holy Spirit
(cf. Luke 11:13b). What they were really seeking in their

prolonged crying out to God was the coming of his Kingdom—more evidence of his sovereign power. Their cry
could be reduced to the simple petition of the Lord's
Prayer: "Thy kingdom come, thy will be done, on earth
as it is in heaven." Like the friend at the door of his neighbor they cry, "Give us this day our daily bread"—which in
another way amounts to the same thing. Or, to use Pauline
language, they wanted more evidence of God's working
"for good with those who love him, who are called according to his purpose" (Rom. 8:28)—more assurance that
God was for them and not against them (v. 31).

The kind of answer they sought may be illustrated from
the testimony of Paul, who could point to the series of
deliverances that punctuated his life from the time he
escaped over the wall of Damascus in a basket until he
escaped the shipwreck on the island of Malta. It was not
one deliverance or two or half a dozen, but many—spread
over a generation, so that a cynical observer might be
moved to consider whether the apostle lived a charmed
life. But to Paul, his deliverances were the farthest re-
moved from the possibility of chance. They were too consistent, too ordered and enduring, to be anything but the
action of God in his life. Nor was Paul merely concerned
with his own survival—with saving his own skin. This
would have been abhorrent to Paul, for he knew that in
every deliverance the purpose of God was being served.
If that purpose could have been better served by suffering,
persecution, and martyrdom, that to Paul would have been
equally a sign of the action of God, as it certainly was for
the Christ whom he followed.

But beyond these signs there was the future Kingdom of
God, to which they pointed and of which the elect needed
to be assured. This was the consummation of the ages—
the vision the prophets foresaw when they spoke of the

wolf dwelling with the lamb and the leopard lying down with the kid and the nations beating their swords into plowshares and their spears into pruning hooks (Isa. 11:6; Micah 4:3), and the vision of the Apocalypse, which told of the time when God shall wipe away every tear from their eyes and death shall be no more, neither mourning, nor crying (Rev. 21:4). The elect yearn for the assurance of this hope. If they can have this assurance, then the time of their tribulation will seem brief. "For this slight momentary affliction is preparing for us an eternal weight of glory beyond all comparison, because we look not to the things that are seen but to the things that are unseen; for the things that are seen are transient, but the things that are unseen are eternal." (II Cor. 4:17–18.) When Jesus assured them that God would vindicate them speedily, his assurance had to do not only with such signs as Paul experienced in his ministry but with the foreshortened hope of the consummation, which would be both judgment and redemption.

This would be the answer to the cry of all those who in the Lucan source looked for the deliverance of Israel (cf. Luke 2:25, 38; 19:9; 24:21; Acts 1:6), as it would be to the deep longing of the human heart for a deliverance that surpassed the achievement of justice. In all this, those who had seen Jesus both from afar off and from the nearness of his presence would feel the tension between what they knew him to be and the world in which they lived. It would only deepen the poignancy and meaningfulness of their cry and cause them to press forward the more earnestly. Having once tasted of deliverance, they could not refrain until they found themselves at the ultimate feast. Christ himself would be both the one who prompted their cry (prayer) and the one who answered it. He would be their justification.

X

The Quest for Status
(Luke 14:7–11)

Now he told a parable to those who were invited, when he
marked how they chose the places of honor, saying to them,
"When you are invited by anyone to a marriage feast, do not
sit down in a place of honor, lest a more eminent man than
you be invited by him; and he who invited you both will come
and say to you, 'Give place to this man,' and then you will
begin with shame to take the lowest place. But when you are
invited, go and sit down in the lowest place, so that when your
host comes he may say to you, 'Friend, go up higher'; then you
will be honored in the presence of all who sit at table with
you. For every one who exalts himself will be humbled, and
he who humbles himself will be exalted."

The inclination to claim the highest status irrespective
of the qualifications and rights of others is a stubborn fact
of history exemplified in every field of human endeavor.
In its more conspicuous social manifestations it is correlative with a deep and complex condition of spirit, so that
the outward expression is perhaps of less significance than
the inward state. What Christ observed in those who
sought the chief seats at weddings out of a vain desire for
prominence was not, therefore, an incidental matter relative only to a few exceptional individuals or to the
question of etiquette. Rather, he observed a conspicuous

example of what in wider and subtler ways was a serious spiritual problem. This accounts for his seeming tactlessness in calling attention to the guests' actions and thus to some extent creating what would undoubtedly be a scene. The boldness of those persons to whom he addressed his remarks is indicated by the fact that in full knowledge of the custom of older and more distinguished guests arriving last, they pushed into the seats reserved for their superiors and incurred the risk of embarrassment on being ushered to the lowest and only remaining seats—for the sake of a few moments of prominence. It was a matter of indulging at almost any cost a craving for status irrespective of others, including even the host and the most distinguished guests.[16]

But if this practice was frequent at social gatherings, it was encouraged at a more serious level by the religious leaders of the community, who in spite of their emphasis on holiness and the observance of the sacred law found ways and means of indulging their love of status. The religious ostentation of the Pharisees, for example, was no different in principle from the more vulgar practice of moving forward to take the most prominent seats at social functions. It was only more refined and acceptable because it was practiced within the context of religion. On this point the Sermon on the Mount leaves no doubt in our minds about the identity of those who, when they gave their alms, sounded a trumpet before them; who loved to stand in the streets and synagogues, praying long prayers to be seen of men; and who disfigured their faces that all might see they were fasting. And the scribes were no better. They chose the chief seats in the synagogues and the uppermost rooms at feasts in a manner that suggested a love of prominence not unlike that evidenced in the parable. In particular, they loved to go about in their distinctive robes and to frequent the market places to receive the salutations of the large numbers of those assembled.

It is possible, however, to argue that the action of the scribes and Pharisees was justifiable on the ground that they were witnessing to the faith of their fathers. On this basis, the ostentatious manner of almsgiving, praying, and fasting could be regarded as an attempt to exert a maximum influence upon the people by means of a devotion that was highly explicit. Since the communication of the significance of any religious faith requires an ample expression of its visibility, the scribes and Pharisees were only fulfilling this requirement. In order to command popular respect in the name of God, they had no other alternative than to claim the chief seats at the synagogues and the uppermost rooms at feasts. The wearing of distinctive robes and the frequent visits to the market place to receive the salutations of men were necessary to impress men with the fact that there was a ministry of God in their midst. That is to say, it could be argued that the ostentation of the scribes and Pharisees was justifiable on the ground of religious outreach in the community, indeed as a form of religious education or even of missionary activity. Out of such a conviction it could be asked: Why shouldn't religion sound a trumpet and advertise itself? Why shouldn't it shout its message from the housetops?

In an age in which the foundations of faith are threatened as they were in the days of the scribes and Pharisees, why should there not be more praying on the street corners to be seen of men? Why not more fasting, with evident signs on the faces of the faithful? Why not more frontlets and robes and salutations? If in the modern age we are particularly desirous of visibility, and believe, as the advertisers affirm, that the church must compete with all those agencies eager to sell their products, how can we avoid ostentation? Does the man of faith not have to thrust himself forward into the forefront of public life and claim as it were the chief seat of attention as frequently as possible? Does he not have to be sensitive to his status and to that of his church in a society in which an inordinate emphasis is placed upon status and the competition associated with it? For the sake of the gospel does he not have to covet both for himself and his church the highest status?

In the last analysis, does he not have to acknowledge that under the circumstances of modern life the scribes and Pharisees were right? Does he not have to admit that what they did is a common pattern of conduct inculcated into modern youth so that in a figurative sense they are taught to choose out the chief seats? If they are unsuccessful at first, they are not to be inhibited by embarrassment. For whatever may be said by way of qualifying the modern quest of status, its similarity to what Jesus saw in his contemporaries and admonished them against is too great and its influence upon the church too subtle to be dismissed as a matter irrelevant to the teaching of this parable.

Jesus recognized, however, in what subtle ways the visibility of religion may be transformed into a vain display and self-righteousness into a presumptuous assertion of status before man and God. Religion which in these respects becomes a means of securing prominence and of contributing to worldly recognition gradually defeats itself as those to whom it ministers discern its lack of love and ultimate concern. Its hypocrisy is too transparent to deceive for long even the average man, who gradually learns to distinguish true religion from that which merely advertises itself.

In the parable, Jesus reverses the whole direction of emphasis. "When you are invited," he says, "go and sit in the lowest place, so that when your host comes he may say to you, 'Friend, go up higher'; then you will be honored in the presence of all who sit at table with you." In this saying the emphasis parallels what we find in the Sermon on the Mount, in which Jesus reverses the emphasis from the ostentation of the scribes and Pharisees to that of the secrecy that comes of humility in the presence of God. "When you give alms, do not let your left hand know what your right hand is doing, so that your alms may be in secret; and your Father who sees in secret will reward you. . . . When you pray, go into your room and shut the door and pray to your Father who is in secret; and your Father who sees in secret will reward you. . . . When you fast, anoint your head and wash your face, that your fasting may not be seen by men but by your Father who is in secret; and your Father who sees in secret will reward you." (Matt. 6:3, 6, 17–18.)

In thus advocating humility, Jesus was advocating only what he himself was exemplifying in his life and ministry; for of all those characteristics which depicted his role as the Suffering Servant of God, it was his meekness and lowliness of heart that was the most significant. This is one of the reasons why his earliest followers so readily applied the familiar prophesy of Isaiah to him as its fulfillment: "He was despised and rejected by men; a man of sorrows, and acquainted with grief; . . . oppressed, and . . . afflicted, yet he opened not his mouth." The apostle Paul, when, in his letter to the Philippians, he appealed to those beloved people to appropriate the mind of Christ, selected the same characteristic as virtually an epitome of the meaning of the incarnation. "Have this mind among yourselves, which you have in Christ Jesus, who, though he was in the form of God, did not count equality with God a thing to be grasped, but emptied himself, taking the form of a servant, . . . and being found in human form he humbled himself and became obedient unto death, even death on a cross." (Phil. 2:5–8.) How seriously Paul and his associates regarded the appropriation of such Christlike humility as characteristic of the Christian life and ministry may be seen in their acceptance of its costly effects in their own experience. "When reviled, we bless; when persecuted, we endure; when slandered, we try to conciliate." (I Cor. 4:12–13.) This norm was derived from the life and ministry of Jesus himself—who exemplified that fundamental humility which in the Old Testament characterized the people of God. It is at once obvious, therefore, why Jesus was sensitive to the glaring examples of religious ostentation of his day. A feeling of pride as a result of engaging in the service of God and a desire to exploit this service for the sake of recognition—indeed as a medium of self-expression—can mean only, according to him, that a man's heart is not right in the sight of God.

It cannot be assumed, however, that the meaning of humility is simple and unambiguous, and therefore unsusceptible to misinterpretation and misunderstanding. For it is evident that the one word "humility" has many meanings, some of which are contradictory, and as derogatory to Jesus and to the faith of his followers as it is possible to imagine. Not to recognize this fact would be a serious mistake, based as it is upon the dubious assumption that any exhortation to be humble is self-explanatory to the hearer. The reason for some precaution may be illustrated with reference to certain psychical and social perversions of humility that are falsely attributed to the Christian faith out of a failure to understand its essential nature. In the first place there is the tendency to confuse true humility with various distortions and weaknesses of personality—with timidity and shyness, with a fear of attempting any task because of an inclination always to remain insignificant, with apathetic quietness, with docility and even drowsiness. In more extreme forms these weaknesses may include a debasement of the self that comes of losing heart and accepting the most menial tasks as though one's lot in life were merely that of a treadmill, to be trodden upon by all those bolder spirits willing enough to exploit the opportunity. At this stage they may even involve surprising forms of self-punishment which are characteristic of a deeply ingrained hostility and which are always, to a greater or lesser extent, conducive to asceticism.

In the second place there is the tendency to confuse true humility with the slave mentality of those persons at the bottom of the social scale who rationalize their hard lot and transform it into a virtue. They are humble both because it makes it easier for them to accept the unsatisfactory conditions under which they live and because their taskmasters find that the inculcation of such an attitude is conducive to social control. The fact that Jesus and his disciples were more or less identified with the peasant class (people of the land) has naturally encouraged this conception, which sees early Christian humility not as something to emulate but as a form of social pathology to be avoided.

If the meaning of Christian humility is to be properly understood, it will be important to recall the familiar text, "Every one who exalts himself will be humbled, and he who humbles himself will be exalted," and to remember the reference point in respect to which the exaltation or humility occurs. An appreciation of this reference point is vital because it is possible to be exalted or humbled in respect to many things—for example: in respect to one's opinion of oneself, to the requirements of the community, to a philosophy or an ideology. Indeed, there are as many kinds of humility as there are reference points to which the individual may respond. In view of the variety, it has to be emphasized that the only reference point for true humility is God himself, so that the text should properly read: "Every one who exalts himself in respect to God will be humbled, but he who humbles himself in respect to God will be exalted." On this basis, it may frequently happen that the humbling of oneself before a reference point that is spurious and possessed of no valid authority over one's life is not only a false humility but in actuality an exaltation of oneself over against God, which is deserving of condemnation.

On the other hand, the humbling of oneself before God means a response to a reference point that is beyond the scope of change and decay. It does not restrict one's allegiance to the passing moods and moments of history and to the implicit authority of each. These can pick up and can cast down not only the individual but also whole societies and civilizations as the restless waves of the sea toss their debris up and down. For the uncertainty of the passing phases of exaltation (feeling of superiority) and of humility (feeling of inferiority) is as hard to endure as the concealed falsity of these vulnerable reference points. In other words, he who humbles himself before God is enabled thereby to stand upright before men without fear or desire of favor—he is free from them in order to be free for them, as we see for example, in the case of the prophet Jeremiah, who at first cringed before the impressive power of his contemporaries. In his fear he cried: "Ah, Lord God! Behold, I do not know how to speak, for I am only a youth." But he was humbled before God and freed from the bondage of fear with the assuring words:

"Do not say, 'I am only a youth';
for to all to whom I send you you shall go,
and whatever I command you you shall speak.
Be not afraid of them,
    for I am with you to deliver you, says the Lord."
                                            (Jer. 1:7–8.)

But it is ultimately Christ on the cross who defines the reference point in respect to which Christian humility derives its meaning. Around this reference point a new definition of humility is given. This humility comes of the love which is the ethos of the cross and of the whole initiative that culminated in it, and which, in the exquisite language of the hymn, "is patient and kind, . . . not jealous or boastful, . . . not arrogant or rude, . . . not irritable or resentful, . . . bears all things, believes all things, hopes all things, endures all things" (I Cor. 13:4–5, 7). It is this love which forbids the follower of Christ to indulge in the ostentation of the scribes and Pharisees and of the self-advertised religion popular in a secular age interested primarily in visible results and quick success. It is this love which forbids him to confuse the afore-mentioned distortions and weaknesses of personality, and the slave mentality of social pathology, with true humility—unless perchance such love (*agapē*) itself is suspect in a power-crazed, sin-sick world.

There should be no illusions about the popularity of such humility—particularly since it revolves around the Crucified One as its definite center. It will always be difficult and subject to misunderstanding. He who exemplifies it in his life will not infrequently be suspected of ignorance, of having no eye for status, and of having had a questionable upbringing. Suspicions may be aroused about his social sensitivities as his love breaks across those distinctions which are popularly accepted. He may even be hated for his humility. At this point it should be clearly understood that real humility is not the popular quality it is commonly represented to be—as if everyone loved a humble man. For there is a false humility, which the proud are always pleased to recognize in others—the humility that listens when the proud sound their trumpets, and that steps aside when they push themselves ahead.

When, however, a Christ-centered humility arises out of its source in love, it comes as a great, liberating, creative power in the life of any person, involving a reorientation of his motives, a disruption of his neurotic defenses, and a shattering of false securities—all in the interest of the freedom of the spirit. This humility results in exaltation—the proper affirmation that comes of the negation involved, in a manner not unlike that in which Easter follows the cross. If this seems strange to us, it is probably because we have always regarded humility as, on the whole, consistently negative and without having any necessary relation to such an amazing possibility. But here we are dealing with an exaltation which, like the humility associated with it, is not essentially moralistic or psychical but eschatological, and in which the action of God is decisive. It is simply another way of speaking of the Pauline analogy of the believer as one who is not only crucified with Christ but raised with him. And since God is acting in the believer's life in such a manner, the succession of exaltation and humility is not a dialectic of history according to which exaltation tends to create humility and humility tends to create exaltation, so that each rises or falls according to its particular phase. It is the strange dialectic of freedom, according to which the action of God is correlative with the manner in which the heart of man affirms or denies him.

XI

Totalitarian Faith

(Luke 14:28–33)

"For which of you, desiring to build a tower, does not first sit down and count the cost, whether he has enough to complete it? Otherwise, when he has laid a foundation, and is not able to finish, all who see it begin to mock him, saying, 'This man began to build, and was not able to finish.' Or what king, going to encounter another king in war, will not sit down first and take counsel whether he is able with ten thousand to meet him who comes against him with twenty thousand? And if not, while the other is yet a great way off, he sends an embassy and asks terms of peace. So therefore, whoever of you does not renounce all that he has cannot be my disciple."

Throughout the New Testament there is a clear and consistent emphasis on the cost of discipleship. Men are attracted to the faith not when the requirements are made easier and are adjusted to popular demand but when they are made difficult—so difficult, in fact, that they can be described only as ridiculous and by every ordinary standard, impossible. Men are torn up by the roots, their old loyalties ruptured, their possessions sacrificed, and their outlook so changed that they find joy in a course of life that is comparable to being put to death. Moreover, they are left no alternative. They are left no other way of becoming disciples. There is no way by which the requirements can be relaxed according to time and circumstance

121

and the needs of the individual who is called. Disciples are not permitted to believe that there are degrees of discipleship, and that only the more courageous may be expected to attain to such a superlative stage. In every case, without respect to persons, the same costly requirements obtain.

It was to emphasize the necessity of costly discipleship that these two parables were particularly designed—each phrased in the form of an extended question.

"For which of you, desiring to build a tower, does not first sit down and count the cost, whether he has enough to complete it? Otherwise, when he has laid a foundation, and is not able to finish, all who see it begin to mock him, saying, 'This man began to build, and was not able to finish.'" A farmer was planning the erection of a tower for the purpose of guarding his property—probably his vineyard, since during the harvest season, marauders were apt to rob him of his fruit. The problem was one of cost. If he began to build only to discover that his funds were insufficient to finish it, he would become an object of ridicule in the community. His neighbors would laugh at him.

The other parable is of a similar nature. "What king, going to encounter another king in war, will not sit down first and take counsel whether he is able with ten thousand to meet him who comes against him with twenty thousand? And if not, while the other is yet a great way off, he sends an embassy and asks terms of peace." This man was a small tribal chieftain who planned to attack a neighboring chieftain. The problem is one of serious risk, in which a miscalculation could mean the loss of everything. For if it is important to count the cost before building a tower lest by failing to finish a man be ridiculed by the community, it is infinitely more important to count the cost before going to war, lest by failing to win it be necessary to sue for peace on the enemy's terms and be subjugated to him.

As these parables suggest, Jesus was having difficulty with enthusiasts. His difficulty was not with critics like the scribes and Pharisees, who were suspicious of his actions and waiting only for an opportunity to denounce him. It was with sympathizers, would-be friends, and overly zealous followers, who without understanding the meaning of discipleship or without counting its cost were interested and ready to serve him. One contributing factor was undoubtedly the extent of his ministry to the restless multitudes who were poor and often destitute and therefore only too ready to follow anyone with a promise of better things to come. Under these circumstances, it was only natural for them to follow him with undisciplined enthusiasm. Their enthusiasm, moreover, according to the Sermon on the Mount, could complicate the final judgment. Even at the end, Jesus would have to disown those whose unwarranted confidence in their spiritual achievements would prompt them to declare, "Lord, Lord, did we not prophesy in your name, . . . and do many mighty works in your name?" (Matt. 7:22).

The problem emerges with greater clarity in the case of individuals who are either committed or attracted to him but who have not counted the cost. The most conspicuous is the man who volunteers for full-time service with a zeal that seems to indicate that he is ready to go anywhere, at any time, under any circumstances: "Lord, I will follow you wherever you go." But his assertion of unconditional commitment is exposed for what it is worth by Jesus' rebuke: "Foxes have holes, and birds of the air have nests; but the Son of man has nowhere to lay his head" (Luke 9:58). He is not ready to accept the insecurity that discipleship involves.

Further, there are those prospective disciples who seem willing enough to follow but who, when Jesus calls, are quick to seek concessions at the critical point of commitment. The one must bury his father, the other bid farewell to his family—requests natural and necessary enough, but for this reason all the more useful in evading the imperative of God. For these and others who recoil at the cost of discipleship, Jesus had a further illustration of the nature of their conduct as meaningful as that of the tower builder or of the king planning for war. An irresponsible disciple is like a plowman who, after he puts his hand to the plow, keeps looking back instead of ahead, as if he could plow straight without his eye on the mark and a willingness to finish the furrow to the end of the field. (Luke 9:59–61.)

It is clear from this, as from the two parables themselves, that Jesus wished to emphasize the adverse consequences of irresponsible discipleship. For he provides us with a serious, evangelical version of the old and undeniable truth that a thing half done is worse than a thing never begun. The foolish plowman meandering around the field in a mixed-up fashion would earn the ridicule of the community even more than the farmer who failed to finish his tower for want of funds, thereby revealing his insolvency in spite of a prosperous front. Moreover, a king rashly attacking his neighbor without considering the fact that his neighbor had twice the number of men (twenty thousand) would be a fool whose blundering could end only in the subjugation of himself and of his people. The emphasis upon confusion, ridicule, and disaster is Jesus' way of indicating the consequences of easy discipleship. It is consistent with the fact that Jesus never indulged in indiscriminate exultation over any inquirer who expressed a willingness to follow him, as if his ability to say No! had been paralyzed and all that mattered were the number of names he could add to his list.

On the contrary, he seems to have had a deeper reason for caution, which has been less appreciated until of late, when defections from the faith have awakened us to the possibility that the easier we make things for the disciple, the more he will despise us for it in the end. Inoculation with what has been described as "cheap grace" seems to develop an immunity to genuine grace, so that some of the worst enemies of the faith in modern times have had their beginning within the faith. Illustrating as it were the logic of the empty house that is swept and garnished, their last state is worse than the first (Matt. 12:43–45). This fact suggests that easy discipleship eventually contributes to a strange hardening of the heart, which is costly in a different sense and not unlike the phenomenon to which The Letter to the Hebrews refers. "For it is impossible to restore again to repentance those who have once been enlightened, who have tasted the heavenly gift, and have become partakers of the Holy Spirit." (Heb. 6:4–5.)

In order to understand the emphasis on costly discipleship, it is necessary to recognize that costly discipleship derives from the total claim Jesus laid upon the prospective follower. If an appropriate metaphor is possible, this claim is not unlike the call to military service, in that the recruit is required to offer all that he has and to be uprooted from the normal course of life. All other loyalties are to be subordinated to this one loyalty—failing which, the other loyalties are to be sacrificed. At every stage, the total claim that is a function of the peculiar authority Jesus possessed is inseparable from the question of his identity (Christology) and the finality of his mission (eschatology). He claims the disciple because he is his rightful Lord. The metaphor of the military is only a way of suggesting that as the Lord of life and death, he has the first word and the last word, and that this is what qualifies the totality of his claim.

It is inevitable that the singleness of purpose inherent in such loyalty should endow it with a characteristic intolerance which the ancients recognized as setting it apart from loyalty to other religions and as making it more provocative of persecution. In all subsequent periods of history, and no less in modern times, this loyalty has been an offense to those whose tolerance envisages a variety of religious syncretism. As a result, the disciple is involved in conflict in which he has no option but to participate. "Whoever does not bear his own cross and come after me, cannot be my disciple." (Luke 14:27.) This means that the cost of discipleship is always potential martyrdom and not infrequently actual martyrdom involving the kind of witness which in the modern as well as the ancient world is described by Tertullian's words: "The blood of the martyrs is the seed of the church." It has to be emphasized that no Christian has counted the cost who has not seriously inquired of himself whether he is prepared to be put to death for his faith. Real discipleship always has this potential quality, no matter how much the believer may ponder how he would act in a time of mortal crisis. It always has within itself the spirit of which martyrs are made.

But the military metaphor has to be qualified further lest it appear too negative and perhaps authoritarian, and therefore suggestive of a regimentation of the disciple that would be foreign to the freedom he has in Christ. It must be emphasized, therefore, that the total claim laid upon the disciple is the claim of love—"the love of God in Christ Jesus our Lord." It is the love that is patient and kind, the love that never ends (I Cor. 13:4, 8), the love from which nothing can separate us—"neither death, nor life, nor angels, nor principalities, nor things present, nor things to come, nor powers, nor height, nor depth, nor anything else in all creation" (Rom. 8:38–39).

With these characteristics, this love is certainly not ordinary love, nor love as a quality or function considered apart from its living subject, the lover. It is the action of God, who is love, and who, in the Lucan parables, is represented in the compassion of Jesus for the poor, the despised, and the outcast—and at the same time in the resistence of Jesus to the proud and the irresponsible. It is this strange love, identical with the freedom God takes in a man's life through Jesus Christ, which explains the unconditional nature of a man's commitment and why he bears the cross; for he cannot let go of the love that will not let him go. This is why the sacrificial life though costly, is essentially positive and possesses a distinctive quality and purpose specifically related to the identification of the disciple with Christ. The disciple's sacrifice is not to be confused with other forms of sacrifice that do not derive from this identification. The careless modern habit of equating the bearing of the cross with those sacrifices which all men eventually experience in one form or another—hardship, affliction, misfortune, domestic burden, and the rigor of exacting duty—has no basis in Scripture and only distorts the meaning of discipleship.

There is another reason for the totality of the claim Jesus lays upon the disciple. This has to do with the nature of the conflict in which he is engaged. Because of the fact that the enemy lays a total claim upon those whom he would recruit into his service, there is no alternative but for the Lord of the disciple to do the same. No partially committed effort will suffice against a foe who never does anything by half measures and whose strategy is to win a total victory. Nothing less will do when, to use the language of the Ephesian letter, the disciple is contending not against flesh and blood but against principalities and powers, against the world rulers of this present darkness, against the spiritual hosts of wickedness in the heavenly places; there is no alternative but to take the whole armor of God (Eph. 6:12–13). The introduction of such a description of demonic powers to indicate the nature of the conflict in which the disciple is engaged is not inappropriate in the present age, when the totalitarian spirit is so characteristic of the secular world. It is present not only in those political and economic forms in which it is obviously the predominant force but in those forms which, though denying it, secretly espouse it in the conformity and loyalty typical of the "organization man."[17] It is not that the present age is exceptional in this respect but rather that in its boldly technological spirit it exploits the worldly pretension of ultimacy that has always been the most serious competitors of Jesus Christ.

The disciple must therefore know what he is doing. His discipleship is never a calling to which the surrounding world is indifferent, much as the world may at times appear to be indifferent. His task, if not pursued with the utmost commitment, is doubly condemned by those who are always happy enough to see it fail. If the failure of the farmer to complete his tower could only earn the ridicule of the community in which he lived, the failure of the disciple to complete his task will earn the ridicule of a much larger community, which might otherwise have respected him for his integrity and persistence. If the failure of the king could only bring disaster, the failure of the disciple will bring a greater disaster, such as always comes of irresponsible militancy on the part of the Christian who fails to assess the power of those against him or who creates enemies of those who might have remained his friends. The disciple who in the name of Christ mounts his horse like the fabulous Don Quixote and rides off to tilt at windmills makes mockery of the serious militancy of the church. In the warfare of the spirit, waged for the eventual possession of the whole man, victory will not be won by foolish adventurers, armchair strategists, camp followers and dilettante supporters, or soldiers of doubtful loyalty. Along the battle line of the spirit, no decisive action is possible with a motley crowd of mercenaries.

The strategy of Jesus demanded the opposite—a minority of well-disciplined, seasoned, totally committed combatants, ready for any assignment and willing to suffer and die. He focused upon the few for the sake of the many because his approach was selective rather than inclusive. This practice was in harmony with the divine strategy by which Israel was called out from the nations for the sake of the nations, and it was the same strategy by which a remnant was called out of Israel for the sake of Israel when through disobedience and hardness of heart she had spurned the prophets. It was the same strategy exemplified in the warfare of the spirit as Gideon displayed in his attack on the Midianites. Out of a large assemblage of potential warriors, all the fearful were at once dismissed. Of the ten thousand that remained, only three hundred were chosen. By their courage and tactics he was able to accomplish what the original thirty-two thousand evidently would not have accomplished (Judg. 7:1–8). Similarly, Jesus saw the hope of the future in the few rather than in the many—a few disciples carefully prepared, a few selected who would remain faithful to the end. This method was more than strategy or policy in the secular connotation. It was the way of the Spirit, the mystery by which the purpose of God seems to be fulfilled with sinful man. In like manner, the future of the church lies with the few rather than with the many. Her true history always consists of the history of significant minorities—the few in every age who have counted the cost and won the crucial victories. Her hope lies in selectiveness and not in inclusiveness. At the practical level, this will mean insistence upon fewer but more deeply committed members, fewer but more adequately qualified ministers—each disciple must know not only the meaning of the faith but the nature of the enemy confronting him and the cost of discipleship as well.

Associated with the parables of the tower builder and of the king planning for war are certain sayings that suggest some of the directions costly discipleship takes (Luke 14:26, 33). There are other sayings that belong so naturally to these that they must be included to complete the directive (Luke 12:4–5; Rom. 12:20–21; Mark 10:43–45; Luke 22:24–27). None are properly regarded as laws definitive of legalism but they are expressions of the deep imperative of the heart within the freedom of faith. They will be stated positively instead of negatively, so that the costliness of discipleship may be recognized for what it confers as well as for what it removes.[18]

First, the disciple finds his satisfaction in the joy of his calling, so that he needs no extraneous source of honor and prestige to build up his confidence. He requires no source of satisfaction other than the nature of his work and of the life to which he is committed, within which the grace of God as divine action is the implicit source of the self-validating character of his calling. Consequently, he is fascinated by it and interested in it at the same time that he is aware of its abiding significance. As a result, he is fortified against the inward restlessness that erupts into vanity and that seeks its satisfaction in the honor and fame of the world. He sees through the vanity that jostles for position and is jealous of its prerogatives. For he has accepted the role defined by the saying: "Whoever would be great among you must be your servant" (Matt. 20:26).

Second, he knows that real wealth is not to be purchased with silver and gold. Money is no substitute for the things that are true, honorable, just, pure, lovely, and gracious, just as it is no substitute for the peace of mind and soul that comes of unconditional surrender to Christ —of laying down one's weapons at his feet. By the surrender of all other securities than that security represented in the acceptance of the cross, the disciple is freed from an idolatrous enslavement to possessions. The neurotic need of making a god out of money and property— or out of anything that belongs to him—is broken. Nor is he overanxious about what he will eat, drink, or wear—a concern that would otherwise leave him exposed to the greatest variety of worldly appeal. In some instances, as with the rich young ruler, it may be necessary for the disciple to sell all that he has and give to the poor, so great has been the idolatrous acquisitiveness. But whatever the case, the disposition prevails that a man's life does not consist in the abundance of his possessions (Luke 12:15).

Third, the disciple is one who has learned to love—the most difficult possibility confronting the human being. It determines more than anything else his eligibility to be human. He has learned to love because he has only one love—a love that, with singleness of heart, is capable of comprehending all, not a love that, with a plurality of likes and lusts, is essentially chaotic. Hence, he is protected against the risk of loving people, particularly his own, in the wrong way. Accordingly, he is no captive of the clan. He is not absorbed or imprisoned by family relationships so that these become his ultimate loyalty. The familiar injunction leaves him no room for compromise: "If any one comes to me and does not hate [but prefers] his own father and mother and wife and children and brothers and sisters, yes, and even his own life, he cannot be my disciple" (Luke 14:26).

Finally, inasmuch as the disciple has accepted the cross with the risk it involves, he is enabled to seek others in a manner unconditioned by the fear of what they may say or do in respect to him. Instead of being confined to those who think and act in the same manner as he, and who are bound together by their mutual likes and dislikes—as any clique exemplifies—he breaks out of this bondage to love those against him, including even his enemies. Consequently, he is neither fearful of force nor disposed to exploit its use, nor does he cringe before the man of power who can kill only the body. In all his dealings, he renounces retaliation. "For it is written, 'Vengeance is mine, I will repay, says the Lord.' . . . 'If your enemy is hungry, feed him; if he is thirsty, give him drink.' . . . 'Do not be overcome by evil, but overcome evil with good.'" (Rom. 12:19–21.)

From these familiar characteristics of discipleship the costliness of the sacrificial life of the believer is evident. To receive honor and recognition without succumbing to vanity, to have possessions without being possessed by them, to love one's own people without idolizing them, to be involved in the use of force without depending upon it or fearing it in the hands of others—these are the signs of the strange and costly task of discipleship in the present world, which at the same time is indicative of the Kingdom of God. These are the signs of the hidden leaven that in the end will leaven the whole of life, fulfilling the first commandment of the Decalogue, which in turn fulfills within itself all other commandments. Impractical though such discipleship appears to be from the immediacy of a secular point of view, it is in the end the only life that is practical. But in such obedience the disciple walks by faith and not by sight—praying always that God will give his Holy Spirit to fulfill in him what humanly speaking is always impossible.

XII

Synopsis

The Religious and the Irreligious

The opponents of Jesus differed sharply with him over the religious and the irreligious. Their attitude was qualified by the unity that obtained in matters religious and political. Although not necessarily expressed in overt, political action, their religious objectives tended to assume political form—if not in the historical present, at least in the eschatological future. As this pertained to the scribes and Pharisees, it signified that their ardent devotion to the law was at the same time a manifestation of national interest. Their zeal for holiness contributed to the achievement of their further objective. Only as they exemplified such zeal did they believe that God would bless their nation and deliver it from its enemies—not only from the conqueror without but from the renegade within.

On this basis, an irreligious countryman was in principle unpatriotic. He was a hindrance to holiness. For the cultivation of holiness was in the national interest, particularly of a people who regarded themselves as the elect of God, called to be holy as he is holy. The logical consequence was an exclusive attitude toward those persons classified as sinners, not only in the narrower category of moral offenders but in the broader category of those whose occupation and social position tended to make them indifferent to religious tradition.

In contrast, the attitude of Jesus was one of compassion. Instead of holding the irreligious in contempt and avoiding their company, he mingled and ate with them. His action was prompted by that concern for the poor, the despised, and the outcast which characterized his ministry and manifested his desire to seek and to save the lost. As a result, he found himself in sharp conflict with the scribes and Pharisees, who saw in his action a dangerous form of freedom that threatened established religion. Branding him with the uncomplimentary title "Friend of tax collectors and sinners," they questioned his authority and came to the conclusion that no compromise was possible.

Only a lack of historical perspective, however, would fail to recognize that the exclusive attitude represented by the scribes and Pharisees contributed to the preservation of the identity of their people. As an expression of holiness, it protected them against various forms of paganism that would have assimilated them into oblivion. For the emphasis on holiness which defined the religious over against the irreligious, was representative of the struggle of a people—indeed of a remnant within its midst—to preserve its historical and God-given uniqueness. The struggle from within against the irreligious was to the scribes and Pharisees only another phase of the struggle from without against worldly powers that would have overcome them. It was not unlike the struggle of a modern nation against those subversive individuals in its midst whose way of life is of one piece with the threat of subjugation from without. It is only as we appreciate this fact that we can understand the concern of the scribes and Pharisees over Jesus' fellowship with sinners. To them he was one who, though claiming to be religious, was associating with those subversive individuals whose influence was detrimental to the historical existence of their people. Claiming to be holy, he was, according to their understanding of holiness, encouraging unholiness.

If the Sadducees were more materialistic and readier to compromise with foreign ways of life, it was not because their ultimate objective was much different in principle from that of the scribes and Pharisees, often as they found themselves at variance with them. For the Sadducees were always concerned to preserve their priestly prerogatives and to maintain the Temple cult, presumably for the glory of Israel. To them, as to the scribes and Pharisees, Jesus was an object of suspicion, particularly as his activities were seen more and more as encroachments upon these prerogatives. At the same time, as we see from the role that Jesus assigned to the priest and the Levite in the parable of the good Samaritan, he was not unmindful of the inadequacies of the representatives of the Temple cult. Indeed, the extent to which he challenged the cult is indicated by the fact that in the end the Sadducean priests were the most aggressive in procuring his crucifixion.

The crucial consideration dividing the religious from the irreligious was the meaning of holiness. In this context, holiness was more than a noumenal or an ethical category, in view of the manner in which religion and politics were unified. Instead of an abstract conception considerably divorced from the actual situation, as often emerges from studies devoted exclusively to the nature of holiness, it is preferable that our conception be consistent with the fact that holiness was implicit in the unified social, religious, and political complex. In other words, we should think of holiness as a category that inevitably serves all these aspects and at the same time represents the ethos of the established order. As already indicated, this is especially the case in a society that conceives of itself as the elect of God and as enjoined by religious sanction to be holy. Such holiness, by embodying within itself as its primary significance a unique principle of separation, was accepted as the popular dynamic of particularity, whether it pertained to the priests in the Temple, the scribes and Pharisees, or any devoted son or daughter of Israel.

It is not surprising, therefore, that the question of holiness, more than any other, became the crucial issue which throughout the ministry of Jesus divided him from his opponents. The whole conflict of the religious versus the irreligious resolved itself into this question. This fact is evident from an inspection of the various controversies of his ministry and of the points of difference that provoked them. The observance of the Sabbath as a holy day, and more especially the purification rites, which in preponderance of detail had a larger place in Jewish tradition than any other matter, were the main subjects of controversy. Although Jesus' critics frequently posed for him various questions on points of law, which were not infrequently trick questions with dangerous implications, these questions were largely incidental to the main consideration of his authority and the way in which it contravened accepted presuppositions of holiness. It was the freedom he assumed in respect to holy things—the Sabbath day, the Temple, the law, the tradition, and the forms of separation that each involved—that was the most provocative. This is the reason his opponents took particular exception to his fellowship with sinners.

At this point, the conclusion suggests itself that the issue of holiness over which Jesus and his opponents were so sharply divided must be seen in the context of social control. The importance of seeing it in this context must not be obscured, however, by whatever else the meaning of holiness may rightly or wrongly include, for this conclusion also follows from the peculiar unity that obtained between the religious and the political. The ruling class in Israel, no less than in any modern society, had to be able to convince itself and the widest possible constituency that it possessed superiority. This, of course, is seldom, if ever, an easy task, because it requires a form of conditioning and of institutional enforcement that is never only a rational achievement. A ruling class must really believe in its superiority. Its assurance cannot be merely a device consciously adopted for the purpose of securing power.

Historically, one of the most effective of the various means of social control has been an emphasis on holiness, which as a power more especially possessed by priests and kings of almost every land and era has reflected the aristocratic spirit. The more awe, majesty, potentiation, or mana a king or a priest possessed, the more respect he commanded and the better control he exercised over the people, particularly if this control was reinforced by a doctrine of divine right. In the more extreme forms, which Israel resisted, this doctrine amounted to a form of deification. But whatever the form or the extremity of expression, holiness, in so far as it contributes to social control, resembles a high transmutation of the ethos of the "better" class. This kind of holiness has been especially useful the more its possessors could avoid creating the impression that their superiority was to some extent a rationalization of the politics of power.

For this purpose, as has already been suggested, the secret had to be concealed from themselves if it was to remain concealed from their subjects. And what better way of effecting this desirable end can be conceived than for priest or king to disavow the possession of holiness in and of himself, claiming only the acceptance of it as a gift, albeit a gift that significantly enough remains within his control and subject to manipulation according to rule? This does not invalidate whatever else the nature of holiness may or may not include. It only calls attention to the peculiar exploitation to which holiness has been historically susceptible and indicates that, in those societies where religion and politics and other interests have coalesced, such exploitation seems to have been especially operative.

But holiness is not the prerogative of priests and kings. It may become the prerogative of a group like the scribes and Pharisees, whose role in first-century Jewish society represented a high degree of social control. As those devoted to a conception of holiness according to which the potency could be attached to or detached from persons, parts of persons, and items of property, they had within their grasp an effective means of social control, particularly as the irreligious were ready to recognize and respect their piety. At the same time, it assured them as a party of that inner cohesion and awareness of uniqueness which always makes for concerted action as a pressure group. Therefore, anyone like Jesus, who together with his disciples had a different conception of holiness—*ipso facto* had a different conception of social control, of society, and of that order (Kingdom) which God purposed to establish—would also have a different conception of God.

The Crisis of Love

It is upon this background that the question of the scribe, which introduces the parable of the good Samaritan, is so highly significant. For it is not an incidental question of only theoretical interest but one that emerges from the social and religious situation as indicative of an inward and inescapable contradiction of its ethos. It is therefore a much more crucial question than is usually credited to the scribe. It is one of those essential questions which a society is always asking itself directly or indirectly, when its conscience is ill at ease. As a member of the Pharisaic party, devoted to the practice of holiness and to the avoidance of spiritual defilement, the scribe would be sensitive to this question. For how could he be a neighbor and always remain separate? Could he restrict his neighborliness only to the circle of his associates? If not, then to what extent and under what circumstances could he go beyond that circle? In other words, the emphasis on holiness, with its principle of separation, would by its very nature accentuate the problem of neighborliness, with its principle of identification. Each principle would involve a peculiar risk to the other. To become a neighbor would involve the risk of compromising holiness, whereas the practice of holiness would involve the risk of compromising neighborliness.

But the question is more than one of personal relevance only to the scribe. In a larger perspective, it is of relevance both to Israel and to the church in their respective conceptions of themselves as elect peoples—and for this reason distinguished and separated from the world. Election by its nature creates the question of neighborliness in a unique and unavoidable form for Jew and Christian alike. This goes back in a special way to the emphasis each places upon the transcendence of God, who in this respect is separated from his people and his created order and who is therefore one with whom a relationship of love is impossible by means of the simple expediency of identification. Love will involve by its very nature, of course, some kind of identification, but in this case it will always be conditioned by separation. In the case of the love of God for man, God remains God, and man remains man, with no absorption of the one into the other.

It can be appreciated, therefore, why under these circumstances the meaning of neighborliness so readily becomes problematic. If the love of God for man is conditioned by separation, then the love of man for man consequent upon God's love is conditioned by separation. Everything will depend on how the conditioning is conceived. If it is conceived in a totally negative manner—with holiness turned inward upon itself and upward to God, accompanied by a defensive attitude toward those beyond its limits—a crisis of love is signified. Love is rigidly circumscribed and limited in the interest of holiness and all that holiness procures, with the result that the question of the identity of the neighbor becomes acute. In the case of the society of which the scribe was representative, we would have inferred as much from the negativism of those in the parables whose conduct was anything but neighborly despite their holiness. We would have recognized it had the scribe never asked his question. The indifference of the priest and the Levite who passed by the wounded man on the other side, the blindly condescending attitude of the Pharisee toward the tax collector, the resentment of the elder brother toward the father and the prodigal—these are the examples that suggest a crisis of love implicit in the religious life of the participants. In a more secular form, not so obviously related to this negative conception of holiness, although indicative of social discrimination and possibly of the Sadducean temper, we have the same problem in the callousness of the rich man to Lazarus and in the self-centered ambition of the farmer who pulled down his barns to build greater barns. In each case there is a failure to accept responsibility for a neighbor, and therefore there is a crisis of love, inasmuch as the acceptance of responsibility for another is one of the principal criteria of love.

From the emphasis that Jesus laid on the need for a radical love that is inseparable from loving God with the whole heart, soul, strength, and mind, it is evident that he saw in the crisis of love the primary sin. Even sexual sin for him was sinful not because it was sexual but because in another way it also represented a crisis of love. But the need for a radical love meant at the same time a corresponding adjustment in the conception of holiness, for the crisis of love was as much a crisis of holiness, inasmuch as each involved the other. In other words, it was in the realm of holiness—in the higher range of the mind and spirit—that he detected the locus of the crisis of love. It is here, where the possibility of social control is finally determined and qualified and where for this reason the greatest potential of influence is to be found, that we see the awful significance of sin in relation to man and God. Here it is that sin under a negative form of holiness can be represented by a conception of deity that is but an obstruction to ultimate concern for others and a barrier to genuine neighborliness. As a result, the spiritual pattern of a whole generation, surprisingly, may be determined by what happens in the minds of a few—the few who happen to be in effective control, including most significantly the custodians of the religious or ideological tradition.

This at once suggests that our consideration of the question of the neighbor must not be divorced from the context of social control to which the understanding of holiness is always susceptible. For becoming a neighbor involves not only a risk of defilement but a loss of influence and prestige and of the superiority necessary to social control. If this seems strange in view of the common conception that neighborliness means the opposite, it need only be observed how easily identification leads to loss of control. Parents who identify too closely with their children, teachers with their pupils, and rulers with their people, soon lose control over them. Familiarity, intimacy, too common a relationship, lead to loss of respect and eventually of co-operation. A line of separation must always be maintained as a precaution against this possibility, and the line is all the more effective if defined and consolidated in terms of laws and institutions. But the inevitable result of such precaution is that the crisis of love is built into the social structure and perpetuated by it. Holy institutions tend to enshrine it within themselves and to conceal its real and essential character.

Because Jesus appears to have seen this result, the orientation of his mission and message was in this direction. His message was not directed solely toward the inner, subjective life of man, as if the solution to the crisis of love were possible within the realm of feeling without disturbing those social institutions and patterns of interest by which the social control of the elite was established. His message was not a subtle form of adjustment to the established order, according to which the individual changes only his inner life and nothing of the outward order itself—as much modern evangelism, moralism, and mental hygiene would have him do. Instead, it was oriented toward the whole man—toward his inward and outward life, toward his individual and collective life. Therefore, it challenged social institutions and patterns of interest and conduct as much as it challenged the inner life, because the crisis of love pertained as much to the former as to the latter.

This will at once suggest why Jesus did not merely heal the sick but dared to heal them on the Sabbath day, why he did not merely appeal to the lost from a distance but went and ate with them and by so doing violated the laws of holiness. For the law of the Sabbath and of religious purification had been so formulated that it embodied within itself in institutional form the same crisis of love that we see exhibited in the negativism of those persons in the parables whose conduct was anything but neighborly. In other words, there was an inner contradiction between the original purpose of the law as the scribe rightfully defined it (Luke 10:27) and the way in which it had been interpreted and expressed in institutional form. In its institutional form, the law had been conceived primarily as a means of social control rather than as an instrument in the service of love. As holy law, it was but an expression of the same negative idea of holiness.

The Revolt Against Holiness

The crisis of love created by a form of holiness that permits men to escape from responsibility is not overcome by a denial of all holiness. Such a denial, so widely advocated today as a reaction against a form of religion that permits men to escape responsibility for their neighbor, as though faith in God were an obstacle to social justice, is not the answer. In other words, to eliminate the principle of separation, which is implicit in every form of holiness, and to do it in the interests of an unlimited identification, will not facilitate genuine love. It will not make men more responsible. The complete removal of the

circle within which the scribes and Pharisees circumscribed themselves or, what amounts to the same thing,
its expansion to include the whole of humanity, will not
overcome the crisis. An unrestricted, promiscuous, pantheistic togetherness that would eliminate the separation
represented by transcendance—in other words, an atheism
that would get rid of a transcendent God for the promotion of love, the love of humanity—will not bring about
a genuine love for the neighbor.

The fact that Jesus did not become a people's man in the
sense of a complete identification of himself with the poor,
the despised, and the outcast is tantamount to a rejection
of this view. His protest was neither a mere agrarian protest against the urban interests of scribes, Pharisees, and
priests nor an ancient equivalent of a revolutionary zeal
for a classless society. Instead, he resisted the temptation
to become a people's man and merely the mouthpiece of
their protests and a patron of their interests. Had he
identified himself with the common people in such an
absolute manner, there would have been no necessity on
his part for seeking after them as a shepherd his lost sheep
or a woman her lost coin. The fact that he was so emphatic about the necessity for the search is evidence that
he had not identified in such a complete manner with
them.

Complete identification would have meant a denial of
any necessity for the search. It would have meant that he
recognized no distance between himself and them definitive of their lostness. He would have been lost with
them, if under these circumstances lostness could have
any meaning. The shepherd would have been as lost as
the sheep he was seeking, the woman as lost as the coin.
In other words, Jesus maintained a line of separation between himself and those he sought, even though in his

seeking he desired identification. This means that there was a holiness implicit in his mission and message to the lost, which for this reason was different from the holiness of the scribes and Pharisees. Indeed, the conflict that divided him from them involved a conflict between two kinds of holiness—one that turned inward upon itself and manifested a crisis of love, and another that turned outward to others and expressed, as it were, the solution to the crisis. The difference between them turned on the fact of responsibility. The one desired social control without responsibility beyond itself; the other accepted responsibility but did not insist on social control.

In other words, we have to recognize that there is a form of holiness as necessary to love as love itself is to holiness. Expressed in the most general terms, there is a form of transcendence that is necessary for the preservation of freedom, inasmuch as love and responsibility are categories of freedom. In his freedom to seek the lost, Jesus did not deny his freedom to be himself, having regard to the essential nature of his person. He did not deny his integrity as a person. He did not deny that basic particularity which is ultimately definitive of his uniqueness as an individual. He recognized a necessary polarity between the individual and society, between himself and the society he wished to create, according to which neither the one nor the other should be absorbed. The same polarity defined the relationship between holiness and love, between separation and identification.

The apostle Paul understood this polarity clearly, if we may illustrate briefly from him. He affirms in the most unequivocal manner: "Though I am free from all men, I have made myself a slave to all, that I might win the more. . . . I have become all things to all men, that I might by all means save some" (I Cor. 9:19, 22). In this well-known text, two things stand out clearly and parallel what has emerged from the discussion of the Lucan parables: (1) he is free from all men, i.e., separated from them—holy unto the Lord; (2) he is free for all men, i.e., identified with them—hence all things to them. In such polarity, the first freedom is the condition of the second. He is free from them in order to be free for them. The one freedom is for the purpose of the other, that purpose being the same as Jesus' search for the lost—which in the language of Paul is that he by all means might save some. But the winning of these, the saving of them, is not for the purpose of exercising control over them. It is to make them free and therefore responsible.

If there is any exercising of control over men, it is not a control in the hands of an elite, of a ruling class mediated by a form of holiness which it manages and manipulates, but a control defined by a new form of holiness, a transcendence that secures their integrity. In the language of Paul, holiness consists in the fact that he is a slave of Christ, and, in the case of Christ, in the fact that he is the servant of the God who sent him. But the control arising out of such servitude, which is definitive of individuality, is the condition of that freedom for others which is expressed in responsible love. It is this control at the center which atheism denies in the interest of a control that is completely social and that requires the individual to yield himself from the center to society, at best in the name of an indiscriminate love (togetherness), at worst in the name of regimentation. In other words, the particularity of the individual, which in the thinking of Jesus is secured and defined by the relationship of a man to the transcendent God, who himself is particularized, is completely denied. There are no longer individuals in the essential meaning of the term.

The Search for the Lost

More must be said, however, of the reason why Jesus sought for the lost. It is not enough to say that he was free from them in order to be free for them, for this is only an assertion of the possibility of his seeking them. So we have to begin with the simple observation that in the case of the lost sheep, coin, and son—to take the three most relevant parables (Luke, ch. 15)—the fact that each is lost does not nullify the fact that each belongs. Even though the emphasis falls on the joy of recovery as the main point in these parables, this axiomatic assumption is implied. It is there by the very nature of the analogies adopted. The lostness is not conceived as nullifying the belongingness. The shepherd, for instance, did not allow the fact that his sheep was lost to convince him that it no longer belonged to him. Nor did the woman doubt that the coin still belonged to her, or the father the prodigal to him.

The importance of emphasizing this fact is that it indicates why, in each case, the search was initiated. The shepherd sought for the lost sheep because it belonged to him—because the lostness threatened his ownership. His search was an assertion of his ownership. Similarly the woman's coin belonged to her. She had a claim upon it; therefore she sought to actualize her possession of it. The danger was that she might not find it and that eventually someone else might find it. Likewise, although the prodigal was separated from his father both by distance and by the degradation of the pigpen, the father yearned for his return. The gracious welcome with the gifts of the ring, the shoes, and the best robe symbolized the fact that the father had not rejected the prodigal. It was a reassertion of his sonship.

Expressed in theological language, such belongingness means that the lost were still within the covenant. God's claim was still upon them. His faithfulness was not nullified by the unfaithfulness of man. To use the Pauline text, "Where sin increased, grace abounded all the more." This explains the significant fact that Jesus could say of Zacchaeus the tax collector, as an evident reminder to those who thought otherwise, "He also is a son of Abraham" (Luke 19:9). It also explains the reason why Lazarus the beggar was carried by the angels into the bosom of Abraham. Although he was poor and abandoned at the gate of the rich man and ceremonially unclean by the standards of contemporary religion, he was still a son of Abraham. He and the rich man were still bound together within the same covenant of God, although the rich man did not realize it. A similar fact seems to lie beneath the surface of the parable of the unjust judge, in its reference to the elect who cry day and night unto God. If the elect include the poor and the outcast like Lazarus, Zacchaeus, and the woman in the house of Simon, it means that they also were within the covenant and would be vindicated of God. Salvation was still possible for them. They were not abandoned of God. It was his will to search for them and give them the assurance they earnestly desired.

At the same time, such belongingness interprets the "preciousness" of the lost. This is simply the observation that the sheep is precious to the shepherd because it belongs to him, the coin to the woman because it belongs to her. The sheep and the coin are not precious of themselves independently of the relation of "belongingness" that binds them to their respective owners. The "preciousness" is not a thing-of-itself that has independent validity. This conception of the infinite value of the individual sees preciousness as a relation of man to the Creator rather than as a quality or right posited in man as a possession. The essential humanity of man is a derivative of this primal claim upon him by the Creator. Correlatively, the covenant of God with his people is a fulfillment of this primary claim—a reassertion or a reinterpretation of it, so to speak. In other words, the salvation of his people is but the outworking of the purpose of God from the beginning —stifled and disrupted though it be by sin and by the strange and ultimate possibility of lostness.

By a similar token, such "belongingness" interprets the "lostness" of the lost. It means that the lostness has reference to all that would nullify the claim of the Creator upon the creature—to all that would absolutize the separation between God and man from the side of man. Symbolized by the wandering away of the sheep, by the prodigal's restless desire in the name of adventure to leave his home and father behind, by the elder brother's alienation from his father, by the disillusionment of the rich farmer, and by the torment in which the rich man in contrast to Lazarus eventually found himself—to mention several of the facets of this complex and mysterious possibility—lostness is much more than a moral category. It is much more than a synonym for badness. It is the negative correlate of holiness. It is that "otherness" which is the polar opposite of the transcendence of God. In the present world it is perhaps best symbolized by emptiness and by the dissolution of values, as well as by the violence that inevitably follows as a reaction. In the ultimate sense it is symbolized by such Biblical imagery as torment, fire, or outer darkness—all of which is representative of hell.

In view of these observations, we can see more clearly why Jesus sought for the lost. He sought them primarily because they were human beings, and only secondarily because they were lost. He sought them primarily because they were precious to him, and only secondarily because they were separated from him. Therefore, his seeking did not cease when he found them. His outgoing love did not suddenly stop. His concern did not terminate as if he were saying to himself: "Now that I have recovered my own, there is nothing more to be done. With their lostness overcome, my objective has been accomplished." There was nothing in Jesus of that negativism often found in the proselytizer who, having secured the conversion of the lost, has less interest in them and not infrequently fails in building them up in the faith. Instead, Jesus' seeking was of one piece with the love that continued in the form of fellowship with them. The movement that initially took the form of his search for the lost was now the movement definitive of fellowship and worship. It was the movement that was definitive of the life of the new community into which the lost had been accepted.

Since his primary emphasis in seeking the lost was on the fact that they were human beings, Jesus had less to say of sin. This does not mean that he minimized sin or thought less seriously of the lostness of those whom he sought. It only means that in his search for them the emphasis was on identification rather than on separation. If they did not come to know his love, no amount of emphasis on the consciousness of being lost would save them. The fact that he had less to say of sin merely signified his unwillingness to give it that place in faith and theology whch would leave the way open for the evil strategy of infiltrating evangelism with legalism.

The Meaning of Repentance

Since the return of the lost involves repentance, this fact confronts us with a theme that is fundamental to the mission and message of Jesus and one to which The

Gospel of Luke is especially devoted. This theme, which is conspicuous in the parables, is also illustrated by those noteworthy examples of penitent persons who were attracted to Jesus. It is obvious in the three parables of divine initiative, which focus on the joy there is in heaven over one sinner that repents. It is the chief consideration in the parable of the Pharisee and the tax collector, in which the latter goes down to his house justified rather than the former. In the case of Zacchaeus, of the woman in the house of Simon, and of the thief on the cross, it is definitive of their attraction to Jesus and of their abandonment of a sinful pattern of life. Repentance, moreover, is the subject matter of the familiar saying that those who exalt themselves will be humbled and those who humble themselves will be exalted—a saying that interprets not only the two parables to which it is attached but almost all the Lucan parables, as may be illustrated by the experience of the prodigal, the rich man and Lazarus, and the man who pulled down his barns to build greater barns. The first part of the saying is descriptive of the unrepentant, the second part of the repentant, with the difference between the two represented by their contrasted orientations.

The problem, of course, was what repentance really involved. The opponents of Jesus would readily agree on the essential role it ought to have in the religious life and the importance of recognizing it as integral to faith. The scribes and Pharisees, in common with Judaism throughout the ages and in succession to the prophetic appeal, had much to say about repentance. The rabbinical sources contain many fine sayings on the necessity and efficacy of such a spiritual quality. Apart from the Christian faith, there is probably no other religion that insists as strongly on repentance as Judaism.

But even so, apart from both the Christian faith and Judaism, where is the religion that does not have its form of repentance? Does not every religion have its equivalent of that submission to a higher power or norm which for the individual is representative of humility and which, when he returns to his religion after any deviation, is for it the equivalent of repentance? Does not communism have its equivalent of such submission and repentance, in which its converts confess the sin of having lived according to bourgeois standards and plead for acceptance into the new community? In form, at least, the sincerity of the admission, the emotionalism and the radical change of character and conduct, is at times similar to the most striking religious conversions. The question, then, of discovering significant differences is crucial. So we find it necessary in the case of Jesus and his opponents to inquire how his conception of repentance contrasted with theirs. For they differed with him here no less than over the question of religion and irreligion and the equally contentious question of holiness.

The main point of difference seems to emerge out of Jesus' friendship with tax collectors and sinners and with those generally described as the poor and the outcast. It consists in the fact not that the lost were sought because they had repented but rather that they repented because they had been sought. Repentance was not the condition of his seeking, but the seeking was a condition of the repentance. He had first broken through the restrictive holiness so sacred to his opponents in order to make an effective contact with sinners without waiting for them to repent as a condition of his seeking. Their repentance was a product of his seeking. It was a product of his identification with them. We see it in the case of Zacchaeus, in which the initiative of Jesus in seeking him provoked the crowd to murmur that Jesus had gone to be the guest of a sinner. The repentance, which was so magnanimous in its character, followed the visitation as its consequence. A similar relationship between identification and repentance seems to have obtained in the case of the woman who came to Jesus in the house of Simon the Pharisee. She was of ill repute, and oblivious to the scorn of those about her, but her sacrificial act was indicative of the trust Jesus had previously inspired in her, even though at the time it was a sign of deep repentance. His previous contact with her explained why she had entered Simon's house uninvited and in effect had forced her attention upon Jesus. He had moved her to seek forgiveness and now he forgave her.

The parables of divine initiative presuppose the same sequence of identification followed by repentance. It is clearer in the case of the lost sheep and the lost coin than in the case of the prodigal, because the latter, in coming to himself in the distant land of despair, seems to have taken the initiative. But a closer examination of the story will indicate that the magnanimity of the father was not conditioned by the prodigal's action. For even before the prodigal could utter his words of repentance the father had welcomed him with the joy of unconditional acceptance. Nor should we overlook the belongingness of which the prodigal was conscious while still in the distant land and which, even if it were only a dim awareness awakened by adversity, was enough to precondition his initiative.

Another difference between Jesus and his opponents with respect to repentance was his emphasis on the necessity of it for all—the religious as well as the irreligious, the holy as well as the sinful. It was easy for his opponents, as it is for the unduly pious of any religion—Christian or otherwise—to be convinced of repentance as suitable only for sinners. The prayer of the Pharisee in the Temple, which cited his several works of supererogation but evidenced no acknowledgment of sin, suggests as much. The reference to the ninety-nine who need no repentance could very well have the same connotation—that the religious conceive of repentance only for sinners—but in the absence of indisputable proof we have to consider the less ambiguous passage: "When you have done all that is commanded you, say, 'We are unworthy servants; we have only done what was our duty.'" On this basis, the Pharisee in the Temple should have considered himself an unprofitable servant, and similarly the elder brother in conversation with his father. For no matter how well one may observe the law, the increasing pride implicit in the awareness of the good is never overcome by self-determined effort.

With Jesus, repentance was neither a meritorious act nor an act which in principle was unnecessary for the religious. It was essentially a matter of a man's becoming honest with God, his neighbor, and himself, of his recognizing the truth about each and accepting responsibility in the form of appropriate obedience. Goodness conscious of itself as goodness, and holiness conscious of itself as holiness, prevented this. Each concealed within itself a form of dishonesty. As a result, each conceived of repentance as appropriate only for sinners, because the good and the holy presumably have no sin to confess. Or, if in some measure they do have it to confess, such action is presumably regarded as meritorious, which simply means that the acknowledgment of sin is prevented from becoming serious. In other words, the difference between Jesus and his opponents turned on the fact that in comparison to their conception of sin, his was deep and radical.

If, however, we wish to grasp more clearly what Jesus understood by repentance, we have to consider the theme, germane to the thought and message of the parables peculiar to Luke, that everyone who exalts himself will be humbled, and he who humbles himself will be exalted. This, ostensibly, means little more than the old proverb of pride before a fall and its opposite alternative, especially if understood out of context. But within context, the theme has reference to pride and humility as these words are theologically understood. The decisive consideration is the reference point in respect to which a man is exalted or humbled. This is the definitive point that endows exaltation and humility with meaning and that really determines the meaning of repentance. As such, it rules out repentance as primarily sorrow for sin and emphasizes instead decision and action. A man may sorrow over sin, experience remorse, indulge in self-analysis, and submerge himself in the subjective, but without the decision that begins with insight and carries over into action, it will not become the turning point in his life that genuine repentance always is.[19]

But since it is possible to be exalted or humbled with respect to almost anything—personal ambition, public opinion, parental expectations, the requirements of success, ideological demands—it is evident that there are as many kinds of pride and humility as there are reference points. Consequently, it is all the more important to recognize that the repentance about which we are speaking is theocentric. Thus we should say, "Everyone who exalts himself in respect to God will be humbled, and he who humbles himself in respect to God will be exalted." But what does this mean? How shall we characterize theocentric repentance so that we understand what Jesus meant by it? For God is hardly a reference point in the usual meaning of the term, valuable as the metaphor may be.

The answer that suggests itself from Luke is to equate such repentance with the meaning of discipleship. Since both involve decision and action, both a turning point in the life of the individual, it will not be too difficult to recognize their unity. Repentance is that turning about— that conversion or reversal of life—which is tantamount to the hearing of the call to discipleship. If we understand what Jesus meant by discipleship, we will understand what he meant by repentance. In this regard, there is one thing of which we can be certain. Discipleship is costly. Jesus does not encourage it without counseling the expectant follower to count the cost, which in the wider perspective may mean persecution and martyrdom. Thus we can speak of the cost of repentance.

In other words, repentance is the same as taking up one's cross and following Christ. It is total commitment. It is a new freedom from the securities normal to everyday life—honor, possessions, family and national interests, power and authority. It is the recognition that none of these have any claim to ultimacy or can substitute for God. Such commitment is analogous to military service, in which the individual surrenders his self-interest in obedience to a call which, although involving the risk of death, transcends and fulfills what his self-interest would not only fail to achieve, but if left to itself, would obstruct. In this respect, it is the end of all conduct prompted by the meritorious motivation that presumes to win the favor of God. Since such motivation is a sign of that resistance at the center, which is at the same time a re-sistance to genuine love, we could say that victory over it is nothing other than the birth of love in the soul. It is the end of the crisis of love.

References

1. E. Hoskyns and N. Davey, *The Riddle of the New Testament* (Faber & Faber, Ltd., London, 1931), p. 118.

2. Joachim Jeremias, *The Parables of Jesus,* tr. by S. H. Hooke (Charles Scribner's Sons, 1955), p. 100.

3. Emil Brunner, *The Mediator,* tr. by Olive Wyon (The Westminster Press, 1947), p. 541.

4. J. Jeremias, *op. cit.,* p. 106.

5. Fyodor Dostoevsky, *The Brothers Karamazov* (Modern Library, Inc., 1950), p. 64.

6. William Shakespeare, *Merchant of Venice,* Act II, Scene 6.

7. George Foot Moore, *Judaism, in the First Centuries of the Christian Era, the Age of the Tannaim* (Harvard University Press, 1927), Vol. II, p. 159.

8. J. Jeremias, *op. cit.,* p. 114.

9. Alfred Plummer, *Commentary on the Gospel of Luke,* International Critical Commentary (T. & T. Clark, Edinburgh), p. 419.

10. Voltaire, in E. Brunner, *op. cit.,* p. 447.

11. Colin Wilson, *The Outsider* (Victor Gollancz, Ltd., London, 1956).

12. Flavius Josephus, *Wars of the Jews,* II, 13:6.

13. *Ibid.,* II, 17:6.

14. Oliver Goldsmith, *The Deserted Village,* Line 51.

15. J. Jeremias, *op. cit.,* pp. 35, 127.

16. Vance Packard, *The Status Seekers* (David McKay Company, Inc., 1959).

17. Cf. William H. Whyte, Jr., *The Organization Man* (Simon and Schuster, Inc., 1956).

18. Karl Barth, *Church Dogmatics* (T. & T. Clark, Edinburgh, 1956), Vol. IV, Part 2, pp. 546–553.

19. William Douglas Chamberlain, *The Meaning of Repentance* (The Westminster Press, 1943).